The Last Buffalo Hunter

The Last Buffalo Hunter

MARY WEEKES

As told to her by
NORBERT WELSH

FIFTH
HOUSE
PUBLISHERS

First published in 1939 by Thomas Nelson and Sons, New York
Published in Canada in 1945 by The Macmillan Company of Canada Ltd.

Cover design by John Luckhurst/GDL
Cover painting, *Assiniboine Hunting Buffalo* by Paul Kane, is reproduced
courtesy The National Gallery of Canada, Ottawa

Printed and bound in Canada
98 97 96 95 94 / 5 4 3 2 1

The publisher gratefully acknowledges the assistance of The Canada
Council, Communications Canada, and the Saskatchewan Arts Board.

Canadian Cataloguing in Publication Data
Welsh, Norbert, b. 1845

The last buffalo hunter
Originally published: New York : T. Nelson & Sons, 1939.
ISBN 1-895618-38-X

1. Welsh, Norbert, b. 1845. 2. Frontier and pioneer
life - Northwest, Canadian. 3. Indians of North
America - Northwest, Canadian. 4. Indians of North
America - Canada. 5. Bison, American - Northwest,
Canadian. 6. Hunters - Northwest, Canadian - Biography.
I. Weekes, Mary, b. 1885. II. Title.

FC3217.1.W45A3 1994   971.2'02'092   C94-920009-3
F1060.9.W45A3 1994

Fifth House Publishers
620 Duchess Street
Saskatoon, SK
S7K 0R1

Contents

Foreword

M
ary Weekes's first meeting with Norbert Welsh in August 1931 was entirely by chance. Holidaying at the family cottage in the Qu'Appelle Valley east of Regina, she had been invited by a group of friends to join them in a birthday visit with the eighty-six-year-old Welsh at nearby Lebret. Weekes was intrigued by the blind old man—one of the last surviving Red River traders and buffalo hunters of the old North-West—and when she asked Welsh to tell her about his life, he said he liked her voice and invited her to come back the next day. Almost every day thereafter for the next few months, she commuted between Regina and Lebret, sometimes dragging along her youngest child, and recorded Welsh's tale on a dictaphone. The experience was a labour of love for Weekes, but it was not without its low points; Welsh often drifted off to sleep during their sessions, and sometimes lost his train of thought and fell helplessly silent. By October, however, the process was complete, and the pair signed a formal contract authorizing Weekes to publish the story. Fourteen months later, Welsh was dead.

The writing of the Welsh biography was the first major project of its kind for Weekes, although it was not her first venture into writing. Born in Tracadie, Nova Scotia, in 1884, Mary Loretta Gerrin was educated in the province and then trained as a nurse at Boston City Hospital in 1910. She served briefly as supervisor of nurses at the Boston Psychopathic Hospital before moving to Regina in 1914 with her husband, Melville Bell Weekes, a Saskatchewan civil servant. Weekes continued her professional career in Saskatchewan with the Victorian Order of Nurses, but soon had to give up the work following the birth of the first of three sons. She kept busy, however, by turning her hand to writing short stories—first about nursing and then about the history of her adopted province. In fact, she quickly developed a keen fascination for the Prairies and saw in the Welsh interviews a chance to record a first-hand account of the last days of the great buffalo herds.

Weekes worked on the manuscript during the winter of 1931–32, trying to keep the story as close as possible to the old man's reminiscences. She sent a draft copy—under the original title "The Waning Herds"—to Sir Frederick Haultain, former territorial premier and Saskatchewan chief justice, who kindly penned a brief introduction, and expressed the hope that Weekes would realize a substantial reward for all her hard work. This prediction seemed about to come true when in late 1933 *Maclean's* magazine carried a serialized version of the story. Weekes also submitted the manuscript to a nonfiction contest sponsored by Atlantic Monthly Press. Here it reached the final stages of the competition before being eliminated on the grounds that the story's setting and content were better suited for a Canadian audience. The judge did admit, however, that "there were passages in the story which I simply ate up."

Weekes tinkered with the manuscript over the next few years, drawing upon the formal instruction she received in creative writing at Harvard University for several consecutive summers. In the end, though, she could not interest a publisher in the story, now retitled "The Last Buffalo Hunter," and she started work in 1936 on a new interview project with a former northern trader.

By this stage in her career, Weekes was producing articles, short stories, and poetry for a number of national and regional magazines, but she still had not published a book. That dream seemed one step closer to reality in the spring of 1937, when she reached an agreement with the Canadian Broadcasting Corporation to run a twelve-part radio dramatization of "The Last Buffalo Hunter" starting the following February. This renewed interest in the story prompted Weekes to try once again to find a publisher, and at the suggestion of a CBC

Foreword

executive, she approached Thomas Nelson and Sons of New York. This time, probably in response to the popularity of the CBC broadcasts, the manuscript was accepted.

The Last Buffalo Hunter was released in November 1939, some eight years after Weekes had interviewed Welsh. The book was favourably received; there was even talk of a Braille version. By 1941, however, it was out of print and Nelson had no desire to do a second printing. Weekes was disappointed by the decision—even more so by the sales—and eventually signed an agreement with Macmillan of Canada in 1945 to publish a new edition. But this too was soon out of print and Weekes arranged to have the rights signed over to her in 1951. She apparently planned to place the book with a Saskatchewan publisher, probably the School Aids and Textbook Publishing Company of Regina, which produced many of her other books in the late 1940s. Despite Weekes's best efforts, *The Last Buffalo Hunter* was never released again, and by the time of her death in 1980 it had become a minor classic.

The republication of *The Last Buffalo Hunter*, more than half a century after it first appeared, finally fulfils Mary Weekes's wish of making Norbert Welsh's life story available to a wider audience. And a fascinating story it is. Although born and raised in the Red River area in the midnineteenth century, Welsh had to migrate steadily westward with the disappearing buffalo herds and winter over with other mixed-blood families on the Prairies. The narrative is interspersed with revealing insights into the personalities of the period and the changing life of the mixed-blood and Indian populations, from the ways of the hunt to the coming of settlement. The greatest value of *The Last Buffalo Hunter*, however, is that it is one of few surviving oral accounts of the period and as such, is a testament to Weekes's foresight in seeing that Welsh's story was preserved. As a reviewer of the original edition remarked, it "deserves to be not merely 'prized,' but *read*."

BILL WAISER
UNIVERSITY OF SASKATCHEWAN
1993

Introduction

I met Norbert Welsh for the first time when I went to his home at Lebret, Saskatchewan, with a group of pioneers, to visit him on his birthday. As a comparative new-comer to the now cosmopolitan West, I found it interesting to hear these men of the old North-West who spoke, first English, then French, Cree, and Sioux, re-live their colorful experiences of long ago.

One of the members of this pioneer group had been a clerk at the old Hudson's Bay Trading Post at Fort Qu'Appelle; another had been in the Royal North West Mounted Police garrisoned near the Fort. Norbert Welsh, the oldest member of the group, had been a prominent Red River trader and buffalo hunter.

These men of the old North-West spoke about the Fort at Qu'Appelle when it was the centre or meeting place for Indians, trading parties, and scattered settlers; when it was, in other words, the out-post of civilization in the West. It was not upon the hardships of the early days, however, that the memories of these men of the once "Lone Land" dwelt; but upon the glamour and romance that had heralded the opening of the Saskatchewan country.

But of this group, that meets yearly, the most picturesque figure was Norbert Welsh. The old buffalo hunter was eighty-seven years of age and completely blind, but he had a memory crowded with stories that belonged to the making of the West. He was born on the Red River, the son and grandson of Hudson's Bay Company men. He had gone west when buffalo blackened the plains and filled the valleys of the winding

Saskatchewan. As buffalo hunter and Indian trader, he had seen the herds wane, and had watched them disappear forever. Norbert Welsh was not an educated man judged by modern educational standards, yet he spoke seven languages, English, French, Cree, Sioux, Blackfoot, Assiniboine, and Stoney.

I realized that this blind old voyageur of the plains had a story to tell, so I asked him if he would let me write his experiences. He replied that many people had asked him to tell them the story of his life in the North-West, but that he had never done so, because he was particular with whom he did business, adding that he liked my voice and if I would come the next day, he would tell me about the buffalo days.

This is how the writing of this story, "The Last Buffalo Hunter," which is set forth herewith, in the old trader's own words, began.

MARY WEEKES

CHAPTER ONE

My First Buffalo Hunt

My grandfather was an Irishman; he spelled his name "Walsh." He came to Montreal Island, to the Hudson's Bay Company; there he married a Frenchwoman. Afterwards he was sent west to Fort Garry and worked for the Company a long time, trading from fort to fort, and visiting the North. Later he was postmaster for the Company at Fort Garry.

I was born in August 1845, in a log house on the Assiniboine River, three miles up from St. Boniface. The Deaf and Dumb Institute now stands on this ground. My mother's name was Sauvé; she came from the North and was partly of Indian blood—Swampee.

My father died when I was very young. He had been sick for a long time. When he first took sick the Hudson's Bay Company gave him a strip of land on the Assiniboine River, near the forks of the Red. It was three chains wide and four miles long. He was not able to work the land. My mother had to support the family. She made fine moccasins and fine coats for other women. There were seven children in our family, all small.

When I was eight years old I made up my mind that I would go out and work, so I went to a neighbour—an old soldier, his name was Harvin—and asked him for work. He laughed and told me I was too small to work.

I said: "You have a garden. Put me in there and show me what you want done."

He did. I worked in that garden, weeding, all day. At night

1

my boss said: "If you'll work for me this season, I'll give you your board and one cent a day."

I told him that if my father and mother were willing, I'd hire with him. When I told my parents that I had struck a job, I could see that they felt badly, but they agreed. I was one less to feed.

I worked all summer for Harvin for a cent a day and my board. He was the making of me. He taught me how to do things right. At the end of the first week, Harvin paid me in coppers—six. I gave the money to my mother. The second week, I got six cents again. Other boys that I knew were working for coppers. We gambled. I lost all my coppers. My mother punished me for gambling. That was my last gamble.

At eighteen years of age I joined a trading party and left St. Boniface to go west, buffalo hunting. I was hired to a man called Joseph MacKay, who had ten Red River carts and fifteen horses in his outfit. MacKay got his goods from an Englishman named Bannatyne, a big merchant at that time at Fort Garry.

We packed everything in those ten carts and left Fort Garry on September 10, 1862. On our first day we came to a place called St. François Xavier, eighteen miles from Fort Garry, coming west. This was MacKay's headquarters; he was staying with his father-in-law, Pierre Poitras. We spent two days here, fixing up things for the trip; then we hitched up and travelled as far as Portage-la-Prairie, forty-two miles from St. François Xavier.

We generally travelled all day without stopping, except for two hours at noon to rest and to feed our horses. When we were in a settlement we bought fresh meat, but on the prairie we ate pemmican—buffalo steak pounded with fat—and dried buffalo meat. The two women in the party did the cooking. They made fine bannocks by mixing flour, water, and baking powder together, and cooking it in frying pans before an open fire. We carried butter in jars, and, of course, we had plenty of tea and sugar. Sometimes we could get potatoes at the Hudson's Bay Company's posts.

There were in our party Trader MacKay, his wife and little boy, MacKay's brother-in-law and his wife, and myself. We went on to MacKay's headquarters at Big Stone Lake, near Victoria Mission[1]–this was north-east of Edmonton–and put up there for the winter. It took us nearly thirty days to make the trip.

MacKay's supplies consisted of tobacco, tea, sugar, powder, shot, small bullets, Hudson's Bay blankets, all kinds of prints and cottons, vermilion (lots of vermilion), axes, butcher knives, files, copper kettles, guns, and–the main thing–alcohol, lots and lots of alcohol.

When we got to Big Stone Lake, the boss decided to go buffalo hunting to get our winter's supply of meat. So we made preparations and started.

We made for Father Lacombe's Mission Station on the north branch of the Saskatchewan River. Father Lacombe had one of those Hudson's Bay York boats. We planned to borrow it to transport our supplies across the Saskatchewan River. Father Lacombe was away, but his man, an Indian, lent us the boat. Those boats were very heavy. It generally took seven men to handle one. We took all our supplies across on this boat.

Now we had to cross our carts. We tied each cart to a horse's tail, then made him swim the river and cross the cart. We did not use rope–that would not have been strong enough–but shaggannappi, which is a thong made out of green buffalo hide. It was very strong and pliable.

I took my horse and tied one big knot at the end of his tail; then I took my shaggannappi and twisted it twice around the tail just above and around the knot, and fastened it with a slip knot. I fastened the other end of the shaggannappi to the pole of the cart, then drove my horse into the river. When he got to the other side, the men slipped the knot off his tail and let him go. The men pulled the cart up the bank. The river here

---

1. Author's Note: The Hudson's Bay Company had a post at Victoria Settlement on the North Saskatchewan River about 70 miles below Edmonton. It was established about 1870.

was a little more than a quarter of a mile across. We had five carts of our own, but there were in all twenty carts, as other hunters had joined our party. We put all the carts across the river in this way—twenty of them.

Here is a little story and it is a true one. It was told me by Archibald MacDonald, chief Hudson's Bay Factor at Fort Qu'Appelle. About sixteen years after I crossed the Saskatchewan River in this way, he was driving to Fort Garry in a buckboard drawn by two horses. About eight miles this side of Portage-la-Prairie, at a place called Boggy Creek, he saw, as he went down the hill, a pair of horses attached to a waggon stuck in the creek.

MacDonald called to the man and asked him what he was doing there. The man answered that he was stuck. MacDonald urged him to try the horses again, but the traveller replied that he was tired trying. MacDonald told him that if he would try to help himself he would help him. The man had very light whiffle-trees, so MacDonald threw a long shaggannappi to him and told him to tie one end to the tongue of his waggon.

"Now, I will tie the other end of the shaggannappi to the tail of my horse and he will pull you out," said MacDonald.

"Tie it to his tail! I never heard of such a damn fool that would want a horse to pull with his tail," exclaimed the man.

"Do as I tell you," advised MacDonald. "We will see who is the damn fool, you or I."

The traveller fastened the shaggannappi as directed, tied it twice around the tongues of his waggon, and made a slip knot.

"Now, take your reins, back your horses a little, and when I tell you to command them, you will command them. Go!" shouted MacDonald, and away the waggon went out of the slough, and up the hill. The man threw himself on his knees and thanked MacDonald for taking him and his family out of the bog. He never knew that such a thing could be done, that a horse could pull with his tail, he told MacDonald. Well, I know from experience that what a horse cannot pull in harness he can pull with his tail.

We were now across the river on the south side of the north branch of the Saskatchewan. We were travelling south-west in the direction of the Rockies. We hitched up our horses. We had now about twenty-five carts in the brigade, a man to each cart. We travelled for two days, but saw no sign of buffalo. We were getting anxious as we hadn't much grub with us. But just then one of our scouts, who had started out very early in the morning on the lookout for buffalo, sighted a cow which he shot and skinned; the carcass he brought back to camp on his horse before we were up.

We soon dressed. Each man was given a piece of buffalo meat, which he cooked for his breakfast. We made a big feast. The buffalo scout said that as this had been a lone buffalo, he had shot it. Had he seen a herd, he would not have fired. A shot would have started a stampede.

The next day we came across the buffalo herd, a small one, and each man that had a buffalo horse—that is, a fast runner, one that can run a half-mile a minute—got on its back and chased buffalo. There were fifty or sixty in the herd, and out of these we killed forty-five. We used single and double–barrelled guns, and loaded our guns as we rode. We skinned the buffalo, cut up the meat and packed it in our carts. I was delighted, as this was my first buffalo hunt.

The next morning we started back home. We had enough meat for the winter. It was now two or three weeks since we had left our headquarters at Big Stone Lake. It was the beginning of November and very cold.

When we reached Lacombe, we camped on the edge of the river opposite the Mission. The trouble now was how to get across, because there was ice, in big pieces, floating on the current. The York boat in which we had crossed the river was now on the north side. There was only an Indian at the Mission—Father Lacombe was still away—and there was no man within a distance of fifty miles to help him cross the boat.

We rested beside the river that day. About dinner-time the next day, I asked my boss, MacKay—he was a kind of quick-tempered man and I didn't want him to get excited—if he had a horse that could swim as well as a man. He replied that he had a horse that was a good swimmer and asked what I was going to do. I told him that I would swim the river with the horse. He didn't want me to do that, he said. I answered that I would rather risk my life swimming than stay there. Then I asked him to have the boy bring the horse.

While the boy was gone, I put on very light clothes, drew and lapped the tops of my moccasins over the bottoms of my pants, and tied them down fast. I pulled my belt tight, and tied a red cotton handkerchief over my head. Then I jumped on the back of the horse and we plunged into the river.

When the horse began to swim, I threw myself into the water on the east side of him. With my right hand I held fast to his mane, and with my left I pushed the big pieces of ice that were floating near us away from his back. I kicked out with my legs and swam with all my strength. The horse was a great swimmer. He held his head and neck out of the water, and, because he was cold, he swam fast. When we got to the other side, the Indian at the Mission took me into the house and gave me a well-sweetened cup of tea that he had made ready. He also gave me a piece of pemmican into which saskatoon berries had been pounded. He lent me Father Lacombe's clothes to wear until mine got dry.

When I was thoroughly warm, the Indian and I started to take the York boat across the river. It was hard work for two men, but we got it across. When I got out of the boat, I asked my boss if my efforts satisfied him. He replied that he never expected to see another man do what I had done.

Then we crossed our baggage, meat and stuff on the boat. We left most of our carts on the bank of the river until freeze-up, when we could get them across easily. The others we tied to the tails of our horses and sent them swimming across the river. Then we went back to Big Stone Lake. We had a house rented from a half-breed named Ka-pa-tooch who had two wives. He was a man who had no religion.

MacKay was a regular cavalier of the plains. Full of dash, like all first class traders and buffalo hunters. He always rode a fast buffalo running horse, one of high mettle. He had a rich outfit for his horse—beaded saddle and cloth and fancy bridle with lariat and whip. He cut a handsome figure on his prancing horse. He had fair skin, blue eyes, and wore his long yellow hair in ringlets and curls.

He was the son of John Richard Mackay, early trader of the Hudson's Bay Company at Brandon House and later Beaver Creek, when it was removed to Fort Ellice on the banks of the Assiniboine River. His wife was a daughter of Pierre Poitras of St. François Xavier on the Assiniboine River. She was very fine looking also. Both she and her husband were very hospitable. Their home, whether tent in the buffalo country or cabin in the settlement, was always a gathering place for the leading hunters and traders of the plains—for the aristocrats. We paid attention to class distinctions in those days, and we buffalo hunters and traders thought quite well of ourselves.

But for all his elegant dress, MacKay was no coward. Once he was on a big hunt with a party of Métis and Indian warriors. A brave challenged him to put an end to a wounded bull that was standing at bay ready to charge. "You are called such a brave man," he said, "go now and kill that bull. Put your knife in his heart!"

MacKay galloped to the animal and drove his knife into the bull's ribs. The blade gashed his hand badly when the animal reared. He rode back to the Indian and said, "Withdraw my knife and bring it to me, if you are as brave as you say." The Indian refused. Then MacKay branded him a coward in the presence of all the hunters, and told him never again to make his voice heard in the presence of men.

On one of his trading trips on the prairie—of course there were great camps of Métis and Indians all over the buffalo country running way down into American territory—MacKay heard about a young Sioux boy who was being sold back and forth for alcohol. A lot of Sioux refugees had come up into the North-West Territories from Minnesota after the massacre in 1862. Mrs. MacKay asked her husband to buy this unfortunate boy and to bring him to the MacKay house.

MacKay agreed. He gave a gallon of highly diluted alcohol for the young Sioux. This boy became a useful member of MacKay's family. He was called "Ferris," and only left MacKay when he grew to manhood.

MacKay suffered financial losses in the Riel rebellion, and finally he was a poor man like the rest of us. The late Judge MacKay told a story about Joe's unlucky years. One evening, when the Judge was a young man practising law in Prince Albert, he went for a stroll to the west of the city. Coming towards him was an ox drawing a load of wood. He saw no driver. But when the ox drew near, he recognized Joseph MacKay walking gloomily behind the load, deep in thought. "Hello, Joe," called the Judge. "You appear oblivious to the world. Why are you so gloomy?"

MacKay came out of his dream. Said he, "Well, Jim, I have just been thinking of my happy days, of my grand past—when I rode the finest and fastest of buffalo horses in the hunts. I wanted nothing then. I had everything that a man could wish for, in abundance. Look at me now! I am afoot, behind an ox, hauling a load of wood. I was just thinking how true is that passage in the Scripture which says, 'How hath the mighty fallen!'"

CHAPTER Two

My First Trading Trip

That winter my boss sent me out on a trading trip. He fitted up two dog trains, four dogs on each train, and gave me an outfit of goods worth two hundred and fifty dollars, some dried meat, and pemmican. I had my dogs well harnessed, plenty of bells on them and ribbons flying all over. These dogs were of common breed—we could not get Eskimo dogs—but they were strong. Each dog could pull four hundred pounds and race with it. I had a young Indian driving one team. We went very fast over the plains. Sometimes we would ride on the sleigh, and sometimes we would run beside or behind it.

We took in trade, at that time, buffalo robes, and all kinds of furs, fox, wolf, beaver, otter, badger, and skunk.

When I wanted to buy a robe from an Indian I examined it, and I turned it over. If it was a good one, I told the Indian that it was, and that I would give him *pee-ack-wap-sh*. That meant in Cree about a dollar for a good buffalo robe. If it was not a good one, I would not pay that much.

For one buffalo robe valued at a dollar and a quarter, we gave in trade one pound of tea, which cost twenty-five cents at Fort Garry, and half a pound of sugar which cost five cents.

In trading with the Indians, we sold our tea for a dollar a pound, sugar for fifty cents a pound, and one big plug of T and B tobacco for a dollar. This tobacco cost, in Fort Garry, eighty cents a pound, and there were four plugs to the pound.

Any kind of print or cotton measured to the extension of

9

the arms, approximately two yards, and which cost ten cents a yard, we sold for a dollar a yard. For powder, one pint (two little tin dippers-full made a pound) that cost forty cents a pound by the keg, we got a dollar a pound. Bullets that cost two dollars and a half for a twenty-five pound sack, we sold at the rate of ten for fifty cents.

We had different sizes of Hudson's Bay copper kettles. If an Indian wanted a kettle, we would ask what size, and how many gallons. The gallon size was priced at a dollar and a half, the two gallon size at three dollars, and so on. Vermilion was expensive. We would take a knife, dip it into the tin of vermilion, and what we could hold on the tip of it was worth twenty-five cents. (Later, when I traded for myself, I kept a teaspoon in my vermilion box and gave a teaspoonful for twenty-five cents.) A pound of vermilion cost eighty cents wholesale. Butcher knives cost two dollars and a half a dozen. We sold the large ones for two dollars each, the smaller ones for a dollar and seventy-five cents, and so on down.

South of what is now Edmonton, we came to a big camp of Indians. They saw us coming, and one of the headmen came out to meet us. He invited us to trade in the camp, which was Poundmaker's.

I did not know much about the Indians at that time, but MacKay had told me, "When you get to an Indian camp, they will give you a tent for yourself always. The first thing you do is to give them a little tea, sugar, and tobacco. Then they will make tea, smoke, visit, and tell each other that they ought to trade with you."

I followed this advice. Soon the Indians began to come toward us, the headmen, the women, and the children. They drank tea. They brought their furs. We began to trade.

That was not a very good year for robes as the buffalo were beginning to get scarce, but all the same I made a good trade. I think I must have taken out of that camp twenty-two buffalo robes. I also took ten wolf skins—not coyote but regular prairie wolf—five red foxes, and some dried meat and pemmican. The furs alone were valued at three hundred dollars. My boss had given me an outfit worth two hundred and fifty dollars, but I tell you it did not take much goods to total that amount in those days. The prices of goods were high, and the prices for the furs were low.

I spent two days trading in Poundmaker's camp. Poundmaker's own tent was very large. It was conical in shape, and took sixteen buffalo hides to cover it. The buffalo skins were well tanned, and well decorated with stripes, figures, and animals. There were seven people in his family, and they all lived in this tent.

Poundmaker's tipi was held upright by twenty-four pine tree poles. Let us imagine that I am setting up the tent. Well, I take three poles, put them together, and tie them at one end. Now, I stand these poles up and spread them out at the bottom. Then I take the other twenty-one poles and poke them in at the top with the first three. To one of these poles, I have tied the back of the tent. This pole I place so that the top of the tent fits over the tops of the poles. I spread the tent out around the poles.

Now on a little ladder, which I have placed in the centre of the tent, I climb to the top of the poles, and, lapping the buffalo covering over each pole, I fasten it with a wooden peg every two feet. To the outside poles, which form the door, I fasten the tent. Thus an opening of about two feet is left between the poles for the door.

The tent is now standing on three poles. Now I go inside the tent and stretch every pole outward, until the tent becomes taut. When it is properly tight, I take out the wooden pegs, and, at every pole, I drive a peg into the ground to hold the tent firm and make it wind-proof.

There were about sixty tents, or lodges, in Poundmaker's whole camp. The Indians were mixed. There were some Crees, a few Assiniboines, but very few, and a few Chipewyans. The Indians were always mixed in those big camps. Poundmaker himself was a Cree, but he had a little mixed blood. There were two tribes, the Crees who had pure blood, and the Little Crees, who had mixed blood. Poundmaker was slightly related to me by one of my grandfathers, André Trottier, on my deceased wife's side.

Poundmaker was very quiet. He never visited the other tents of his camp unless he was invited. He did not come to trade himself. I did business with his headmen, who called me *Wa-ka-kootchick*, which meant "Turned-Up-Nose." Poundmaker was a man of good judgment. He was well liked by his men, and that was everything. They had confidence in him, and were contented.

Here is a story about some Crees that belonged to Poundmaker's territory, although not to his band. First, I will explain how the Indians of long ago used to track each other. When they saw tracks of an enemy in the snow, they stepped them out to see how fast he could walk or run. Then they knew whether they could catch him or not. These Crees had seen the tracks of a Blackfoot. So early one morning seven of them went on the war-path. On the third day from camp they came to a big butte, and when they got to the top they saw coming towards them on the trail that led over the top of the butte, seven Blackfoot Indians.

In a few seconds the others saw the Crees, and jumped into a kind of den. This was really a sod fort without a roof, which they had built for protection against a band of Crees in a previous fight.

Now the leader of these Crees was Ka-min-akose. He was a regular brave. I knew him well. I used to trade with him and he told me the story. He had only one eye. A Blackfoot had knocked out the other.

Ka-min-akose told his men that, as he had the enemies trapped, there was no sense in seven Crees dirtying their hands on them. He asked that they let him do the butchering. Well, this was hard on the others, but they had to listen to Ka-min-akose because he was their leader. They agreed.

At once, Ka-min-akose took off all his clothes except his moccasins. It was winter, remember. He then painted his body properly. He used several colors of paint and decorated himself well. Around his neck, he tied a fox skin that he carried. Then he tied a string of small sleigh bells that he had with him around his waist, letting the end hang. Finally he took a big knife—the Hudson's Bay Company used to sell these knives, more like an axe than a knife—and went off to the den, singing his war song.

In Blackfoot he said to his enemies: "Be aware of yourselves now. I'm going to give you fair play. I'm going to butcher you all."

He walked to the hut and jumped in among the Blackfoot Indians. He butchered them all. He had scared them with his big knife.

When I got back to headquarters, my boss said that we had better balance our account to see whether I was in the hole or not. He had given me two hundred and fifty dollars worth of goods, and I had brought back three hundred and sixty dollars worth of furs, which sold later in Fort Garry for a much larger figure. MacKay was satisfied with my trade. He said, "Welsh, I thought I was a good trader, but I see that you are going to beat me."

In the spring we went back to Fort Garry. Now I was not satisfied to continue working for another man. I wanted to work for myself. I was anxious to return again to the plains.

Toward the end of August, when the brigades were outfitting for the West, a man named Bobbie Tait, a Scotch half-breed, asked me how I would like to take another hunting and trading trip to the plains for the winter. I told him that if he would give me good pay I would go; if not, I wouldn't. He asked how two hundred and fifty dollars for the season, first of August to first of May, would satisfy me—everything found. I told him that his offer sounded good if he would keep his word. (He hadn't a very good reputation for keeping his word.) Well, he offered to give me a big outfit of goods and alcohol—lots of alcohol. Let me explain here that when I sold alcohol to an Indian, I took one gallon of alcohol and put two gallons of water into it. That makes it just right for the Indians.

Tait said that since I had been out trading before, he would make me head man over the stock. I knew he was rather unreliable, and was afraid of him, so I asked him if he knew what responsibility that would throw on me.

"Ho!" he answered, "I'll send my brother with you to keep your accounts. As well, I'll send François Sauvé, and his wife and son. Sauvé will look after the outside work, mind the horses, get the wood, and do all the chores. His wife will keep house."

I asked him to let me consider this offer, and promised to give him my answer in two days. I considered the entire proposition. I thought I would not be able to make that much money in Fort Garry, so I decided to accept Tait's offer. We drew up an agreement and signed it. We packed Robbie Tait's outfit on twelve Red River carts and started from St. James for the North-West. I think we must have had two thousand dollars worth of goods, including alcohol. We started about the last of August, 1863, and travelled to the Saskatchewan country, to a place called Round Plains (now Dundurn) along the south branch of the Saskatchewan River.

We got there quite late, about the last of October, so we decided to make this place our headquarters for the season. I told our two men—of course I was the first man—that there was a band of Crees going to hunt buffalo across the Saskatch-ewan to the west. The river at that point lay a little north and a little east.

I told Charlie Tait that I wanted him to go hunting with the Indians, while I stayed and put up a house for the winter. He said that he wouldn't go. When I asked him if he were the boss, he didn't answer.

Then I asked Sauvé, the other man in the party, if he would go buffalo hunting if I gave him an active Indian to help him in the tent. He answered that he was just going to offer to go. I found an Indian to help him, and got them across the river with the Indian hunting party. I made up my mind that, as long as Charlie Tait would not willingly do what I wanted him to do, I would make the beggar work. He was a big man too, but he was lazy.

The next thing I did was to build a store-house out of logs.

Into this I put all my goods, and locked it. Then I built a house and put all of our clothes and housekeeping things into it. We did not sleep in this house as it had no chimney or place to make a fire. We slept outside.

One day, after we had been there for two or three days, an Indian galloped up to my tent. He rode a fine horse. He was well painted with vermilion, and finely dressed in buckskins. His saddle was well decorated with beads.

I spoke to him in Cree, asking where he had come from, and what he wanted. He shook his head and answered in Assiniboine that he did not understand Cree. We then talked in Assiniboine. He told me that he and his band of ten tents were going to camp on the top of the hill. In these ten tents there would be between forty and fifty Indians. It was the Chief of the band that I was talking to, but I did not know it.

I found out by further questioning that his name was Hoo-hoo-sish, or Little Owl. I asked him what he wanted. He replied that he wanted to trade, and wanted to know if I were a trader. I replied that I was, and asked him what he needed. He wanted tea, sugar, tobacco, prints, blankets, and lots of things, alcohol as well, he answered. He said that he had many furs to sell. I told him that I would trade with him. He said that he would tell his people, and he went back to this tents.

Soon another Indian came with a couple of buffalo robes. I asked him what he wanted for them. He had a copper kettle in his hand. I knew that that meant alcohol.

"For one robe give me tea, sugar, and tobacco. And for the other robe you will give me alcohol," he said.

I bought the two robes. His kettle, which held a gallon, I filled more than half full of alcohol, and away he went.

By and by another Indian came with two robes. He wanted nothing but alcohol for them. He carried a Hudson's Bay copper kettle that held two gallons. I examined the robes. I thought, "I will pay him well for these robes. That will encourage the other Indians to come with their furs." He clapped me on the back and said that I was a good man. He was pleased, as he went away, that I had given him so much alcohol.

Soon I heard the Indians singing in their camp. They were feeling very gay. Then four Indians came, bringing four buffalo robes. The trading went on for three days. Then an Indian from another band came and offered himself to me as my protector, my guardian. He said that, as I had a lot of stock, it would be wise to have him take care of me. I could not understand or speak Assiniboine very well, so I decided to have this Indian teach me.

At the end of the third day, about noon, another Indian from Hoo-hoo-sish's band came along with a gallon kettle. He said that the Chief had sent the kettle and wanted me to fill it for him. I asked him where his robe was. He replied that they had sold all the robes that were worth selling. Now they wanted me to fill the kettle with alcohol and give it to them for nothing.

I fixed a well-diluted kettle of alcohol and gave it to him. Then I told him not to ask me again for alcohol if he could not bring robes to trade.

After a while I saw the Chief coming down the hill with three or four of his men. Just before that, I had given my Cree guardian, my protector, a large glass of alcohol to encourage him. I knew that we were going to have trouble with the Assiniboines. But I had given him a little too much. He got light-headed. He couldn't stand his liquor.

The Chief came into my house and said that he wanted me to fill his kettle with alcohol. I asked him for his robe. He said that he had none. When I told him that I would give him no more alcohol for nothing, he said, "If you don't give me a kettle of alcohol, I'll destroy all the robes I sold you. I'll cut them all to pieces."

I told him to go ahead. He pulled out a long butcher knife, and from where he stood at the door made a stab at a half-breed that was visiting me. My guardian caught at the blade of the knife, which gashed his hand and sent the blood spattering about the house.

At this I jumped between the Chief and my guardian to separate them. They were struggling for the possession of the knife. I got my guardian off, shook him, and asked him if he were crazy. He said that he had never had a man talk to him like that before, and threatened to cut me to pieces. I told him to go ahead. At this he pulled out his butcher knife and made a plunge at me. I stood where I was to show the Indians that I did not fear them. They respected a brave man. I let him slash my shirt until it hung in ribbons from my collar. The knife gashed my chest and shoulder so that I carry the scars to this day. I had had about enough of this.

There was a green poplar stick lying within reach on the floor and, knowing the Indian's fear and superstition at being hit by a stick, I grabbed it and yelled to the Indians to clear out of the house because I was going to kill them all. They turned and fled, falling over each other as they ran. About thirty Indians had gathered in, and around, my house, but they all cleared out at my threat.

I dressed my wounds and put on another shirt. I was afraid now that the Indians would come back in larger numbers. I had no protection. I was alone, for as soon as he had seen the excited Indians, Charlie Tait had run away and hidden. I felt tired and hungry, for I had not had anything to eat all day. I had been too busy trading and working with the Indians. It was now nearly dark. I boiled some water in my copper kettle, made tea, and got out some dried meat and marrow fat. I had a combination dinner and supper. Everything was quiet now.

I went to bed about eleven o'clock and fell asleep. About twelve o'clock Charlie Tait came back and wanted to know if I had had anything to eat. I told him that I had, but there was nothing for him. I fell asleep again. Then I awoke to hear an Indian singing his war song outside my tent. I thought, "Are they coming back again?" I had recognized my guardian's voice. Remember, I had two forty-gallon barrels of pure alcohol, and about three hundred gallons of the diluted mixture.

My guardian began to sing:

Ya-ya-ya-ya-ya-yaki-ko-chish na-pa-ka-shoo.
Ya-ya-ya-ya-ya-ki-ko-chish na-pa-ka-shoo.

This meant, "the Turned-Up-Nose is a brave man and a wonderful man." Now, you must understand that we had a parchment door. It was a well-scraped buffalo hide stretched on a frame to fit the door. It shone like a looking-glass. The next thing I heard was a rap on this parchment. When my caller didn't force the door, I knew he had come in peace. I jumped up and asked in Cree who was there. He replied that he was my protector, and that he wanted to come in.

I opened the door and he came in. On his back he carried a big bundle. His wife came in, too, with a big bundle. They went to the middle of the room and laid their bundles on the floor. Then my guardian said, "I am going to pay you for what I did to you yesterday, Wa-ka-kootchick. If you had been a coward like me, we would have butchered each other. You were not afraid. That saved us both."

He gave me robes to the value of twenty-five dollars, buffalo, wolf, fox, and badger. This was to pay for my shirt.

From my transactions with Hoo-hoo-sish's band, I took in trade over four hundred dollars worth of furs. Soon after this the Assiniboines went away hunting. I traded with them in their tents the following winter.

Chapter Three

Alcohol–The Staff of Trade

It was now winter and I had to cross the river to find out what my men, who were hunting buffalo, were doing. The hunting-camp was quite a distance from the river. It consisted of fifty or sixty lodges. The Chief of the camp was One Arrow[1] (Kah-payuk-wah-skoonum). He told me that I had come in good time to see the Indians run a band of buffalo into a pound. We went to examine the pound, for I had never seen one before. It was in a bluff.

I saw what work the hunters had put in. They had shut in a good half acre with trees, and around this they had built, out of poplar logs, a wall about four feet thick. This wall was very solid. I noticed a big poplar tree standing in the centre of the corral. I asked the Chief why they had left this tree. It was for the good Manitou, he said, who would induce the buffalo to come. They would put offerings on the tree, and in the morning there would be a big herd.

Night came. The Chief and an Indian went from tent to tent collecting tobacco, tea, and sugar to give to the scout. He was a fast rider who was going out to ride all night, and to locate and herd the buffalo in the direction of the pound. This man was an expert at herding buffalo. After the scout had gone, the Chief invited me to get a gun, and to be ready to join in the buffalo hunt the next day.

---

1. One Arrow (Kah-payuk-wah-skoonum) was one of the signers of the Forts Carlton and Pitt Treaty in 1876. Spotted Calf, the adopted mother of Almighty-Voice, was a daughter of One Arrow.

Morning came. We had no watches, but we could tell time fairly accurately. It was about eight or nine o'clock when the buffalo were sighted. On the road, which spread out for a mile from the pound, men and women were placed a quarter of a mile apart to jump up and scare, or lump, the buffalo as they were driven into the pound. The pound was soon full, and there must have been a thousand buffalo outside of it.

I was standing on top of the fence looking on as the buffalo came in. I found it droll that the first buffalo that entered the pound went round and round the centre tree in a circle like the sun, and each buffalo that was driven in afterward did the same thing. Now the pound was so crowded that the buffalo could not move. We started to shoot. We had guns, bows and arrows, and butcher-knives. When we got through there were one hundred and seventy dead buffalo in the pound. The buffalo were shared. My men got twelve.

I left my men at the hunting camp and went back to headquarters. Then I set about to make a dog sleigh for going out on trading trips. We had brought oak boards, twelve and one-half feet long and one and one-half feet broad, from Fort Garry for a toboggan. We planed these boards, joined two together, put cross-pieces on, then put one end to soak in warm water. When it became thoroughly softened, we turned it up to form a nose.

There was a band of Indians camping near our wintering-place, and from their outfit I selected four unbroken dogs. These dogs cost about thirty dollars each. My whole outfit—toboggan, dogs, harnesses and bells—cost me about a hundred and seventy dollars. We made the harnesses out of tanned buffalo hide. We made the traces very strong, four ply, and stitched them by hand.

I hitched up my dogs for the first time to see how they would look. Appearance in those days was everything. If a man hadn't a good outfit, he was nothing. It is the same to-day. If a man hasn't a good car, he is nothing. I took my "feathers" and attached them to the harness. The "feathers" were a decoration. This decoration was really a little stick about a foot long, knitted over with yarn of all colors. At the end of the stick there was a woollen knob no bigger than my fist, and to this knob ribbons were tied—ribbons of all colors, red, blue, yellow, black, and pink. The more colors the better. The lash of my whip was about four feet long. It was made out of plaited caribou skin, and attached to a handle. On both handle and lash, I had rubbed vermilion. The whip, too, was decorated with ribbons of all colors.

I stood my dogs in place. Over their backs, I spread saddlecloths made out of brightly patterned carpet. Then I put a string of bells around each dog and strapped it under his belly. I thought they looked very well. After going to all that trouble, I took all their fancy stuff off and put it away.

With whip in hand, I commanded my dogs to go. They wouldn't go. They didn't understand what I wanted. Then I gave them each a lash with my whip. This lash did not affect them, for still they did not understand. I gave them each a second lash under the ears. This brought blood. I struggled with them for half an hour. They kept getting tangled up, and they wouldn't start. At last I got them to go, and I took a little ride around our village—log huts of the traders which were scattered over the plain.

There were about thirty or forty of these houses, all made of logs and plastered with clay. These huts were the winter homes of the traders.

Next morning I hitched my dogs up again to see how they would go, and now they understood what I wanted. It had been a big effort to train them. I always fed my dogs well. I gave them three meals a day, the same as myself. I fed them on pemmican and green meat. My dogs always did well.

Soon after I got my dogs trained, I told my uncle, François Sauvé, who was now back from buffalo hunting, that I was going to One Arrow's tent—in those days on the prairie we'd strike a camp of Indians about every ten miles—to make arrangements with him for trading with his band.

Night came. We had three little kegs that held four gallons each. I directed my uncle to put one gallon of pure alcohol into each keg and fill them with water. The next morning about four o'clock, before the other traders were up, I harnessed my dogs, loaded my alcohol on the sleds, and stole away.

When I got to One Arrow's camp, which was about fifteen miles from my house, I found the Indians looking, and acting, very queerly. They were impudent and bold. I asked One Arrow what was the matter. He replied that a trader had brought liquor to the camp the night before. (It was a trader by the name of St. Germain, who had got ahead of me.) I told him that it would be useless for me to stay in his camp as there would be no business for me.

"Ho!" he replied, "we got this alcohol on tick. Our furs weren't ready. We will pay for this liquor the next time St. Germain comes."

You see this trader was a greenhorn. I told One Arrow that I would stay if he would agree to my terms. He wanted to know them. I explained that I had three little kegs of alcohol, each holding four gallons, which I would give him for twelve good buffalo robes. This, I explained to him, was a snap, as all he ever got from other traders was two quarts of alcohol for one robe, and I was prepared to give him a gallon. He replied that he would have to consult his headmen. I agreed. He stood at the door of his tent and called, "Ke-we-pay-e-tow-then!" which meant that he wanted them to come.

The headmen, twelve of them, came running to the tent. The first headman wanted to know why One Arrow had called them. The Chief replied that it was Wa-ka-kootchick who wanted them. Then the headman asked me, in a very rough manner, what I wanted. I explained that this was my first trip to their camp, and, since he was not feeling very well, I wanted to give him a great bargain.

He wanted to know what I meant by this bargain. He had never heard of one before. Again I explained that I had three kegs of alcohol, and that I wanted four buffalo robes for each keg. One gallon of alcohol for each robe, instead of two quarts, was what I meant by a bargain. He thought that was fine! He put his head out of the tent and shouted. He named his Indians—twelve braves—and asked each of them to bring a good robe.

They came with the robes. I took each robe, shook it out, and examined it well. I piled them up. That was good business. Twelve fine buffalo robes in fifteen minutes. Now I told them to take the kegs, empty them, and bring them back. They did. I was all fixed. I had got ahead of St. Germain after all.

All night the Indians sang. The next morning, the first headman came and asked me how it was that the alcohol they got from other traders made them sick. He could not understand why none of the Indians were sick this morning, although they had, during the night, drunk twelve gallons of alcohol. When I told him that my alcohol was better than that which the other traders sold, he told me that they would not buy again from the other fellows but would wait for me.

I now packed my robes in packages, tied them up, put them on my dog-sled—it made a very high load—and went back to my headquarters. The Indians were satisfied with the transaction. With most Indians a trade was a trade, but not with all.

I made several trips that winter to Indian camps. I got a lot of furs. I had brought this year from Fort Garry, two forty-gallon kegs of pure alcohol. I never took goods with alcohol when I went out on trading trips, because when the Indians got drunk they wanted the goods for nothing. So, on one trip I took alcohol, and on the next, goods.

One night on my return from a trading trip it came to my mind what a bad deal I had made with Tait—the agreement to sell so much alcohol to the Indians. Right there I decided to make the alcohol stronger; that is, dilute it one to two, instead of one to three. I did this. Ho! My Indians discovered the change at once, and wanted to know why the alcohol was more intoxicating. The second barrel was stronger than the first, I told them. To this they said, "Oh! Oh! we understand."

My idea was to get rid of the alcohol as quickly as possible. My conscience was telling me that I was selling too much water. I got rid of the alcohol. My conscience was eased and I felt better. Now I had nothing but the goods to trade and that didn't take long. Spring arrived. About the middle of April a big thaw came. We packed our furs and buffalo robes, and got our carts ready to start for Fort Garry.

All the fur-traders started together. We were a big company, about one hundred and fifty carts, and thirty families. It took us four days to travel from Round Plain to Devil's Lake (now Watrous). We camped beside the big bush that was there at that time.

The Indian bands had a habit of following our camps when we were leaving the plains, and trying to steal the horses that they had traded for alcohol. But we fur traders had a law of our own in the North-West. Before we left the country we appointed a Chief officer and four sub-officers to police the trip. Our Chief this time was Gabriel Dumont, who later became one of Louis Riel's lieutenants in the Canadian North-West rebellion of 1885. He was a fur trader also. At Devil's Lake, three other young fellows and I were appointed to round up the horses and watch them all night. The Indians were still following us.

Oh, it was cold—blowing hard and freezing! I can feel the chill now. Although we couldn't sleep, it was a good thing we each had a buffalo robe to wrap around us. I was lying down on my belly beside the horses, wrapped in my robe. Our orders from Dumont had been that if we saw a stranger to address him in three languages—French, Cree, and Assiniboine—and if he didn't answer, to shoot him. There was a big horse feeding beside me. All at once he put up his head and snorted. I thought, "There is somebody! A dog, a wolf, or a man." It was very dark. I couldn't see two feet ahead. The horse snorted again, and jumped away. I could make out a man crouching and walking on all fours like a wolf. Suddenly he straightened, and went toward a fine horse, a buckskin. Then he bent and began to untie the hobble.

I decided to play this fellow a trick. I put my gun down on the buffalo robe. I trod on my toes so he could not hear me, and while he was busy with the knot, I threw myself on his back, my arms around his body. He was terrified. He called and yelled. He was a great big Indian, and, as I was only a moderately sized young fellow, he almost threw me over.

At my yell that I had an Indian, my companions came. We took our prisoner to Gabriel Dumont's tent.

"Hah! The young fellows have played you a trick," Gabriel told him. He bound him, and kept him in his tent that night.

In the morning Dumont called us—his sub-officers—to his tent. He asked who had laid hold of the fellow first. One of the boys told him that it was I. Dumont told the prisoner that it was lucky I had not done what I had been told to do—to shoot. Then he gave him a little tea, sugar, tobacco, and stuff, and sent him back to tell the Indians of his band never again to try and steal horses from Dumont's camp. He told him that I was a terrible man, afraid of nothing, and that if he came again I would horsewhip him. There is nothing an Indian fears more than a whipping.

We were a very jolly group. We sang as we travelled. Someone would start singing the songs of the trail, and soon the whole crowd would be singing. We sang *Les Adieu* and *Le Braconnier,* and many other songs.

I must have taken in on that trip four thousand dollars worth of furs. We reached Fort Garry on the 25th day of May, 1864. When I came to settle up with Robert Tait, he claimed that I was short sixty dollars. He took this amount out of my pay of two hundred and fifty dollars for managing his fur trading trip. I had not made a mistake about his character.

Chapter Four

I Find My Life Partner

At the end of my second year in the North-West, I felt dissatisfied. I was always looking for something that I could not find. One day before the brigade started for Fort Garry, I took a little ride in my dog-sled around the settlement. On my way I met a girl, the daughter of a trader. She was walking. I looked at her and thought to myself, "By Jove, that's what I'm looking for! You'll be my wife."

Well, I knew where she lived, so that same evening I walked to her house. She wasn't there. I was out of luck. I waited. After a while she came in. My heart began to beat fast. I was sitting on a stool. I asked her if she would come and sit beside me. She did. I asked her if she were engaged. She replied that she was not. I told her that I wanted her to tell me definitely whether she was or not. She answered that she was not engaged. Then I told her that I had been looking for her for a long time, and asked her if she would consent to an engagement with me. She agreed. I told her that when we got to Fort Garry we would get married, that she must not break her promise. This was about the beginning of March. What grand moccasins she made for me! I was sure that I had found the right girl!

When we got back to Fort Garry, I began to make arrangements to get married. I did not have much money. Andrew Burk, my brother-in-law, and Andrew Bannatyne offered to provide a big wedding for me, but I refused to let them. I told them that I would take care of my own wedding. I went to

Bannatyne.[1] I had worked for him before I went trading. I had painted his store, the first one in Fort Garry and still standing to-day—and asked him if my face was good for the price of a wedding dress.

"Welsh, jump over the counter and help yourself," he said.

Well, I got a fine piece of cloth for the wedding dress, and took it to the girl. Her name was Cecilia Boyer.

Bannatyne told me that he had been planning on taking me to Saint Paul with him to look after his cargo of furs, but now I was getting married. I told him that I would make it my wedding trip.

I was married on the 26th day of May, 1864, and three days later my wife and I started with Bannatyne for Saint Paul. Bannatyne put me in charge of the whole outfit. We had three hundred Red River carts loaded with furs. These furs represented a fortune. I sent the carts on three days ahead. Bannatyne, my wife and I followed in our own cart, in which we carried a trunk, containing money and papers, and a tent.

We overtook our brigade at the boundary, the Pembina River. We were thirty days on the trip. When we got back to Fort Garry Bannatyne paid me off. I was to get a hundred and fifty dollars for the trip, but Bannatyne gave me two hundred dollars.

I had worked for Andrew Bannatyne before I went trading. He was the father of James Bannatyne who was, in later years, one of the big men in the public life of Manitoba.[2]

Bannatyne was a merchant and trader who made annual trips from Fort Garry to Saint Paul with an outfit of two or three hundred Red River carts. These carts were drawn by oxen or horses, and were loaded with bales of robes and furs. They returned with a cargo of goods for the consumption of

1. A.J.G. Bannatyne. A big merchant at Fort Garry. Afterwards, a member of Parliament.

2. Extract (appended to text) re - Donald Gunn's letter in minutes of evidence taken before The Select Committee of the Hudson's Bay Committee in London, 1857.

the people around Fort Garry and the outlying settlements, and for trading with the Indians.

The custom was to send the freighters and the carts one day ahead. Mr. Bannatyne and his man, who was butler, fireman, hostler, cook, in fact his general camp manager, followed. These brigades of Red River carts from the North always created quite an attraction in Saint Paul, and every season the people there made big preparations for their arrival. There would be about one hundred men to a brigade of three hundred carts, or one man to three carts. These brigades had to be well manned for protection against Indian raids.

At the American boundary a customs tariff was collected from us. The custom was to send the freighters one day ahead of Mr. Bannatyne. He gave the leader an inventory of all our outfit to be handed to the Customs officer, with whom Mr. Bannatyne would make settlement on his arrival at the boundary. No cash was paid to the Customs on our road into the States. On our return we had to account for any difference between the property shown in our inventory, and the goods and property we brought into the British possessions. If, for instance, we had fewer carts or horses, we must pay a duty on any left behind unless we could show that the horses had died or the carts had been destroyed or worn out. Flour was always shipped—not in bags as now—but in barrels containing one hundred and ninety-six pounds net. I remember that in each barrel there was always a can of baking powder one pound in weight. And again inside this can was a small vial of essence, such as vanilla or lemon for flavoring cakes, puddings and the like. This pound can of powder was enough to leaven all the flour taken from the barrel. And so exactly was the baking powder measured that when the bottom of the flour barrel was reached, the last ration of baking powder disappeared. I think that the baking powder of that time must have been stronger than the article now sold under that name.

The merchant princes of those times lived high. I will give

you a description of the canteen we carried. This was a huge box or chest. It took all the available space that one cart could afford. It was divided into two compartments, one below the other. You lifted the lid of this huge chest, and there were, in well-secured pigeon-holes, supplies of all the necessaries and luxuries of camp life and travel—tea, sugar, spices, cheese, jams, jellies, marmalades, preserves, bacon and canned meats, gun-powder, shot and bullets. And then we had wild game which was plentiful along the trail.

Once before, when I was fourteen, I had made a trip to Saint Paul with Bannatyne. That time, too, we sent our carts on ahead. Bannatyne drove in a cart with our tent, bedding, and money. I travelled on horseback. We had four horses in the outfit. One hitched to the cart, one I rode, and two which ran loose. When we got to Pembina River—this means in Cree, high-bush cranberry,—where the Yankees had their Customs' Office, we stopped for two days to get things fixed up and our waiting carts released.

About noon on the third day, Bannatyne and I started. Bannatyne told me that he was sick, but that as his business was urgent he must press on. He wanted to reach Fort Abercrombie, a distance of over two hundred miles, in two days. There he could catch the stage which would reach Saint Paul before his carts should arrive.

We travelled all day. From Pembina we had to cross a distance of forty-five miles before we reached the Big Salt River. It had rained all day, and was still raining heavily when we reached the river bank. Bannatyne was, by this time, very sick. I went down to the bank of the river to see if we could cross. I saw that the bridge of brush, which the brigade had built, was beginning to float on the rapidly rising river. I galloped back to Bannatyne and told him that if we hurried we could get across before the floating bridge was carried away.

He told me that he was too sick to move, and instructed me to unhitch the horse, put up the tent, boil water in the kettle, and make him a cup of tea as fast as I could. He also directed me to open the canteen, find brandy and eggs, and mix some for him. This I did. He drank the brandy and eggs, and the cup of hot tea. He weighed two hundred pounds. And I had to drag and lift him as best I could out of the waggon, and get him to bed. This sickness that he had was gout.

It was now night. I hobbled the horses. Then I sat before the fire and roasted some dry pemmican, and some fine biscuits that Bannatyne had told me to help myself to out of the canteen. He was a fine man, and offered me everything that he had. As I was eating I grew uneasy. I was only a child, and this was a great responsibility. I thought that if anything should happen to Bannatyne, if he should die, I might be accused of killing him. Bannatyne wanted me to sleep with him, but I was afraid to do that, because my mother had told me that gout was catching.

Morning came. As soon as I awoke, I ran to the river. As I expected, the bridge was gone. My heavens! What was I to do? I built a fire, and put the kettle on to boil. Then I went after the horses. When I had the tea ready, I wakened Bannatyne. He tried to move, but couldn't. He could only move his head. His legs were terribly swollen and black. I propped him on pillows, and gave him brandy and hot tea. I told him that we were in a fix for the bridge was gone. I asked him what we were going to do. I advised him to go back to Pembina as he was getting worse.

"Boy," he said, "it's a good idea, but we can't go back. We must go ahead."

"My God! How are we going to cross the river?" I asked.

Then he told me that I had good ideas, and lots of courage, and he would trust me to get him across. Mr. Bannatyne's faith in me cheered me up. I had felt frightened. Now I took the biggest horse we had, leaped on his back, and made for the river. The horse swam right across. I swam him back. The river was about ten feet deep at this point. How to get Bannatyne across? I prayed to the Virgin Mary to help me. Then an idea came to me.

The Red River cart had a railing on each side. I took a long shaggannappi and wove it back and forth between the railings to make a spring. I spread straw over this to make a mattress. Then I asked Mr. Bannatyne if he could help himself up to this bed. He couldn't move. I tried to lift him but couldn't. At last I got him into a sitting position, and backed the cart up to him. I took a piece of shaggannappi and tied him to the railing of the cart. Then I lifted the shafts so that when I lowered them he would bounce over into the cart. Again and again I tried to lower the shafts, but I was too light. "My God!" I cried, and tried again to force the shafts down. This time I succeeded. Now I had half of his body in the cart. His legs hung over. By a tremendous effort I finally drew him up, rolled him in his blankets, and fastened him to the railings with shaggannappi. I tied him well, so that if we should upset I wouldn't lose him.

After that I hitched the horse to the cart. Then I bridled and saddled another horse, tied one end of the shaggannappi to his tail, and the other to the left side of the shaft to prevent the current from upsetting the cart. I ran the horses into the river. Swish! We went right across and up the bank on the other side. I immediately unhitched the horses, got Mr. Bannatyne out of his wet clothes, built a fire and spread them out to dry. It was a fine sunshiny day. We had breakfast—the best of everything—pemmican with pounded choke cherries, butter, and eggs.

The clothes dry, I packed up again. We drove from Big Salt River to Georgetown, Minnesota, a Hudson's Bay Company's post two hundred miles south of Fort Garry, which was named for Sir George Simpson. An American Company ran a stage line between Saint Paul, Minnesota, and Georgetown prior to 1860. It was now only sixty miles to Abercrombie.

After dinner I decided to make ten more miles before camping for the night. The next morning Bannatyne could move a little. He praised me and thanked me for what I had done. We travelled thirty miles that forenoon, before unhitching for dinner. The stage would be at Abercrombie[3] at six p.m. We had only four hours to get there, but we made it. We reached Abercrombie just as the stage came in. Bannatyne took the stage to Saint Paul, after instructing me to join the first brigade as far as Saint Cloud. In the morning I hitched up, and in two hours had overtaken one of our carts. Pierre DeLorme was the driver in charge of the brigade. I accompanied him to Saint Cloud.

At Saint Cloud I found a letter waiting for me from Mr. Bannatyne. He told me that he wanted me to leave Pierre DeLorme in charge of the brigade, take the train and meet him in Saint Paul. I did. Bannatyne was all right again, and able to walk when I met him in Saint Paul. He was glad to see me. He told me that there was a big circus in town and he wanted me to see it. We went together. Soon after we got into the tent, a big storm blew up, and knocked the tent over. There was terrible confusion. Bannatyne and I were separated, and I found my way back to the hotel alone. Bannatyne came back with a black eye. That was my first and last visit to a circus.

When Bannatyne paid me off, I told him that I had worked for him quite a while, and asked him if I had given satisfaction.

"In everything, Welsh," he said.

I replied that I was glad to hear that because, since I had been good to him, I wanted him to be good to me.

"What do you want, Welsh?" he asked.

Then I told him that I knew what trading was and wanted to trade for myself, that I wanted an outfit—goods for trading. He told me that I was the right kind of man, and that he would supply me with all the goods I needed. This was all to be on credit, for I had no money to pay for them. I explained to him that I would have to see how many carts I could rig out before I took the goods.

---

3. Abercrombie: See Alexander Henry's Journal, Vol. 1, p. 148, Elliott Coues, Editor: "Lt. Col. J. J. Abercrombie arrived at this spot Aug. 28th 1858, where he quartered with troops for the winter of 1858–59."

I managed to outfit three Red River carts, and to get three horses. I had left a two-year-old horse on the prairie before I went to Saint Paul. That made the fourth horse.

Then I went back to Bannatyne and told him that I wanted about five hundred dollars worth of stuff. Bannatyne thought this was too little, that I would not be able to make a profit. But there was no use taking a big outfit when I had no carts, I told him. I packed my outfit and made for the plains. I took no alcohol this trip.

We did not go back to Round Plains, but to the south side of the Souris River, to what is to-day Brandon, Manitoba. We camped on the bank of the river. We expected to find buffalo, but there were none. I didn't make any money that winter. The Sioux Indian tribes, whom we had expected to trade with, were away down on the Missouri River. It was a hard, cold winter, too, so they didn't move about.

One day toward the end of January, when provisions were getting low, I told my wife I would take a circle around and see what I could do. There were about eight tents of us altogether, traders' families numbering nearly a hundred people.

I saddled my buffalo horse, threw some blankets on the saddle in case I had to sleep out, and started off. When the sun was going down, I saw a tent. I made for it. It was the tent of (Musqua) Malaterre, a half-breed. I knew him well. I asked him how much he had in the way of provisions. He said he hadn't any on hand, but managed to get three meals a day by hunting prairie chickens, rabbits, and night owls for the big white owls are fine eating if they are fat. He said there was an Indian camp not very far away, but he was afraid to venture near it, for he was alone with his wife and little boy.

I told him that I was tired—I had travelled forty miles in the deep snow that day—and would spend the night in his camp and in the morning go on to the Indian one. Musqua's wife put the kettle on, and then I saw her take hold of a bird. It was not a prairie chicken, and I didn't think I'd like to eat it. I told her just to boil the water, and that I had plenty of grub with me. She did. She made a good strong cup of tea, and we had something to eat together.

Very early next morning I started for the Indian camp. After two hours' gallop, I came to a small camp of Indians. There were two tents. I knew they would be Sioux, but I called in Cree to ask if there was anybody in the tents. They answered in Sioux. We spoke in Sioux. I asked the Chief if he had any buffalo meat. He replied, "Taw-doo-oota." This meant, "Lots of meat."

I jumped off my horse and said to him, "Ches-e-taw-ka" or "What's your name?"

He answered, "Shoo-pe-wan-ee-cha." This meant, "A man that's got no guts."

I shook hands with him heartily—I had seen this Indian before but did not know his name—made him feel that I was glad to see him, and went into his tent.

I asked him if he would sell his buffalo meat, and how much he wanted for it. He said that he would like to get a Hudson's Bay blanket, and a fathom of cloth to make a dress for his "Noo-ta-kaou" (old wife), and some tea, sugar, and tobacco as well.

I told him I had no supplies with me, and asked him how much meat he would give me for one pound of tea, a pound of tobacco, some sugar, a blanket and a fathom of cloth. He asked me to go outside with him. He picked out a heap of meat and laid it aside. He was giving me good exchange, but I was not satisfied. I saw that he had lots of meat and I wanted more.

I took a hind-quarter and a fore-quarter of buffalo and added it to my heap of meat. I told him that he had not asked me for ammunition. He said he had not thought of it. He took another side of buffalo meat, laid it on the pile, and asked me to give him some flint for it. Flint was used instead of a cap on a gun on the old Hudson's Bay flintlock guns.

I told him I would have dinner with him—I had enough grub left for my dinner—then I would gallop home. In three days I would be back with supplies and take my meat. He said that I was too far from home, that I would not be able to make it in a day. I told him that my horse would take me home that night.

I got home that night. My horse was very tired. He had had nothing to eat except what little grass he had pawed through the snow, and some tender bark that he had been able to chew off the willows and shrubs. We had made the trip of fifty miles through snow and were glad of a chance to rest.

I got up early next morning and went to see my horse. I thought he would be about dead, but no, he was as keen as ever. Brave fellow! I slapped him on the back and told him that I would always take care of him.

I told my wife about my transaction with "the man that had no guts," and said I would take her brother with me and go after the meat while she stayed here with her mother. I coaxed her to stay behind—she was going to have a baby—with her mother who was a good nurse, but she wouldn't listen. She said that she would feel safer with me, so I saw that I had to take her.

I fixed a little tent over a sleigh and made it comfortable for my wife. We got to the tent of Malaterre. His wife, who was a fine woman, a La Pierre, was glad to see my wife. She hadn't seen a woman all winter. I left my wife here and went to Shoo-pe-wan-ee-cha's camp and got my meat.

Malaterre and his wife wanted us to stay with them for a while, so, after starting Malaterre's boy back to my mother-in-law's camp with some buffalo meat, I started to make the tent warmer. I cut a lot of long dry twigs and made a fence four feet high around the tent. Over and around the fence I packed snow. Then I got buffalo robes from the man that "got-no-guts" and stretched them around the inside wall of the tent. The tent was large, about twenty feet in diameter. I made it so warm that we could only keep a little fire on.

We lived there. We used to shoot rabbits, and prairie chickens to make the buffalo meat last longer. One night, the last February, my wife wakened me. She was in labor. My old mother had instructed me how to deliver a baby. She knew that out on the plains women suffered and gave birth to children without any assistance. About sunrise Malaterre's wife and I delivered my wife of a little boy.

In the spring of 1865, when we got back to Fort Garry, I had very little to give Bannatyne, only about four hundred and fifty dollars worth of furs. However, I still had some goods left. When I told Bannatyne that I must be a poor trader to come back fifty dollars in the hole, he laughed and told me not to feel discouraged. He said that if I owed fifty thousand dollars instead of fifty then I might think I was a poor trader. I replied that I hoped to God that I would never owe fifty thousand dollars. Of course I had bought some horses while I was away. I went away with four and came back with nine.

Bannatyne wanted to know what I planned to do now. I told him that I didn't know whether to keep on trading, or to go freighting for him. He advised me to keep on trading. There was more money in it.

I went out and got three more carts, doubled my outfit, and took two hundred and fifty dollars worth of goods from Bannatyne. This made my debt to him three hundred dollars. About the tenth of May, 1865, we started for the plains.

As I travelled on the plains, I bought pemmican and dried meat from the Indians. I travelled in the same direction as the year before, up the Souris River to the Red Deer River and the Missouri. Then I went across country from camp to camp, buying meat. Mostly I traded with Sioux Indians and half-breeds.

I got back to Fort Garry about the end of June. My carts were well loaded with pemmican and dried meat. I sold it all to John McTavish, Chief Factor, Fort Garry. When he heard that I was back from the plains, he sent for me. He wanted to know if I would sell to him. I told him that if the price he offered suited me I would; if not, I would not. He offered to pay me twenty-five cents a pound for the entire load, and to make me a present of a hundred-pound sack of flour and a bottle of wine. I agreed to sell to him. I went to my camp, which was about fifty yards outside the Fort, hitched up my horses and brought my five loads of pemmican to the old Hudson's Bay Fort. We weighed the meat. When the amount was figured out, I had eleven hundred and seventy-five dollars coming to me. I crossed over to Bannatyne's store and paid him my debt of three hundred dollars. I had a satisfactory balance left. I had been away a month and a half on this trip. The gallon of wine lasted me over a year.

We got ready again and outfitted for the plains. This time I took out a thousand dollar outfit of goods. I decided to go back to Round Plain (now Dundurn). We got there late in the fall of 1865. The house that I had left there needed re-fixing. I had my family with me now. I mudded the house, and put all my goods in the store-house under lock and key.

Then I decided to go on a buffalo hunt. Although it was the middle of November there was no snow yet. About thirty families from our brigade started after buffalo. For my share in the first drive, I got fifty cows. The buffalo were plentiful. We just went out on horseback and ran them down. At each race I killed from four to six buffalo. We cut the meat up. Some we dried, and some we prepared for pemmican. Then we packed up our meat and returned to our winter post at Round Plain.

It was now about the beginning of December, so each family drew wood and made provision for the winter. I tell you we had a good time out there in the North-West that winter. At New Year's we had a big time. Each man put up a feast.

One day I would put up a big feast and invite my friends to come. We would dance the old-time dances and the Red River Jig—reel of four, reel of eight, double jig, strip the willow, rabbit chase, Tucker circle, drops of brandy, and all the half-breed dances. There were always lots of fiddlers. Nearly every man could play the fiddle.

Then we would go to another family. I tell you, we had a regular good time. We had lots to eat and drink. Those that wanted to eat, ate, and those that wanted to drink, drank. This feasting lasted about ten days.

Of all the dances among the half-breeds and the traders, I think the Red River Jig was the liveliest. There were some great dancers amongst the traders. In those days everyone danced. I mean, they all danced the step-dances and every-thing. Of course, there were many fancy dances, too, but in the main, the thing was to be able to step it up.

There was what you call a rabbit-chase dance at the end of the dance—or ball. What great dances took place at the old Hudson's Bay posts! In the rabbit-chase dance, the men and women stood in a row. Their partners stood opposite them. One couple danced up and down within the column and parted at the end of it. The woman went behind the women's column, and the man went behind the men's. When they got half-way up the column they stopped, then the man chased his partner in and out of the column until he caught her.

Now, the thing was started all over again, only this time, the woman did the chasing. Pretty good, eh? This was kept up until each partner had had a turn.

I remember another dance. It was called the handkerchief dance. This was the last dance of the ball. A man got up with a handkerchief in his hand, tied it around a girl's or woman's neck, danced with her and then kissed her. But you may be sure it was the girls that were selected. Now the girl had to get up, dance around the hall behind her partner, choose another man, tie the handkerchief around his neck and kiss him. And so it went, until every man and woman had been kissed. This handkerchief dance wound up the ball. Everyone was satisfied until the next ball. And, you may be sure, that wasn't long.

CHAPTER FIVE

A Winter Hunt

few weeks later we started on a winter hunt, just the men. A party of ten started out on our buffalo runners. A blinding blizzard came on. It was about forty below zero, but we kept on. I shot ten buffalo. Then we had to skin the buffalo in the blizzard. We were on the open plain, and had no shelter, but we were not cold. We were no weaklings, we men of the old brigades! I had a man helping me. The first cow we skinned, we cut her open, and to pieces. Then I cut a hole in the tripe. The manure was hot, and whenever our hands got cold, we would run and put them in the manure, and they would get as warm as fire.

At night when we got back to camp (there were three tents of us) my uncle, Charles Trottier, said he would go and find out how many buffalo the other fellows had killed. In our little brigade of fifteen men—five had joined our party since we left home—we had shot eighty buffalo, skinned them, and brought hides and carcasses back to camp. Next morning we packed our meat and hides into jumpers and returned to our headquarters.

On a second hunt that winter, a lot of us, twenty or thirty men, crossed the river. We travelled for two days, but saw no sign of buffalo. Our rations were getting low. Our chief, *Ak-a-pow*,[1] Gabriel Dumont's father, called a meeting. He

---

1. In his Journal, Alexander Henry, the explorer and fur-trader, mentions a Gabriel Dumont, who was at Rocky Mountain House with him in 1810-1811. (See Henry's Journal—Ed. Elliott Coues—p. 634.) The North West

asked us what we thought we should do. There was no sign of buffalo and we were nearly out of fresh meat. One man got up and asked Dumont to propose what we should do.

Dumont appointed four men to get up early in the morning and go scouting for buffalo. One was named to go to the east—more north than east; one to the south-east; one to the south-west; and the other to the north-west. I was named the first, and directed to go to the south-west. That would be in the direction of where Calgary is now, but on the west side of the south branch of the Saskatchewan River.

Dumont told me to go south-west to the forks of the Red Deer River,[2] and south branch of the Saskatchewan. If I hadn't seen buffalo before that, I would see there a big hill which I was to climb to get a good view of the country. Gabriel Dumont was appointed to go north-east. Baptiste Parenteau was sent south-east. He also had to climb a hill. Another fellow, Joseph Azure, was sent north-west.

We got up early in the morning and started off. I had a fine big horse. He could gallop all day. I tied a little lunch to my saddle and rode away. I galloped until I thought, by the sun, that it was dinner time. We could tell time almost exactly by standing and facing the sun. If we could step the length of our shadow it was twelve o'clock. The Indians and traders measured time this way.

I reached the big hill and climbed to the top of it. My friend, One Arrow, had once told me that when I travelled alone I should never go back the way I came, especially if I climbed a hill. If an Indian war party saw me, they would wait at the foot and catch me when I came down.

While I was eating my dinner, I let my horse feed to the end of his halter-shank. All at once he jumped and almost slipped the line out of my hand. Then he snorted. I realized

Company's posts extended south into what is now American Territory. Dumont probably accompanied Henry on his trip to the Mandan Indians, prior to his visit to Rocky Mountain House.

2. Red Deer River empties into Red Deer Lake about 35 miles east of Hudson's Bay Junction. The old trader was very clear in his statement that these men travelled on courses 90 degrees from each other.

that there must be something wrong somewhere, but I pulled the horse up and went on to finish my dinner. When I was tying up my little bundle, the horse jumped and snorted again. All at once my hair raised on my head, just as if I had a chill.

I pulled my horse up, bridled him, and threw on the saddle. Then I took my fourteen shooter, my repeating rifle, and put fourteen cartridges into it. I looked at my belt to see how many more I had. There were thirty. That made in all forty-four shots. I jumped on my horse and put my feet in the stirrups. I faced the muzzle of my gun ahead so that I could draw it instantly. I thought to myself, that, with forty-four cartridges, I could put up a good fight if attacked by Indians. At this time the Blackfoot Indians used to raid the Crees.

When I got on my horse I glanced towards the ravine that faced me to the west (it ran from the south branch of the Saskatchewan near the forks of the Red Deer), and something glittered across my eyes like a glass. I had left my spy-glass behind, but I could make out objects in the ravine that looked like deer heads. I started downhill in the direction of these objects. This was contrary to the way I had come up. When I got to the foot of the hill I drove my horse at a gallop in the direction of these objects.

Soon the horse snorted, reared, and turned around to the direction from which we had come. I pulled him right again and gave him a lash. He leaped forward, reared again, and almost threw me. I thought now that I had better do what the horse wished, since he sensed danger and I was alone. To tell the truth, I was a little afraid, although I was prepared to put up a good fight.

I turned and started back home. I held my horse back as well as I could. He was a buffalo horse and wanted to race. He had, although we were half a mile away, scented the Indians. On my way back to camp, I saw, in the distance, an old buffalo bull pawing the ground and making the dust fly.

We all got back to camp. I was the last in. The Chief asked Gabriel if he had sighted any buffalo. He replied that he hadn't seen a hoof. Parenteau answered the same. Azure had seen no sign. Down he came to me. I had quite a story to tell about my experience on the hill with my horse, and about the old bull that I had seen. One Arrow and his man were in our brigade. He said that the sight of the old bull pawing the ground was a good sign, that by noon the next day we would be overrun with buffalo. He told me also that it was lucky I had had a good horse, else I would have been shot by the Blackfoot band. The looking-glass, he explained, had been flashed by them to lure me on.

About five o'clock the next morning, I got up to see about my horses. After my experience of the previous day, I was afraid my horses might have been stolen by the Blackfoot Indians.

I could see buffalo all over. There were thousands and thousands of them travelling in the direction in which I had seen the bull. There was not one herd, but many. Our Chief decided that we would have breakfast before we did anything. He went from tent to tent and gathered up all the food. We had a good breakfast, and by ten o'clock were ready to chase the buffalo.

Two or three men took a herd. That afternoon twenty-five men shot three hundred buffalo. Buffalo never came very close to camp. They would smell us, bunch together, and move away. They seldom came nearer than two or three miles.

The next day we went after the buffalo again and killed four hundred. All around us, as far as we could see, the plains were black with buffalo. The prairie seemed to be moving.

There was one thing that I did not like about that hunt. I saw hundreds of buffalo, during that week, slaughtered for their hides. The whole carcass was left to rot on the plains. One time I saw three fine fat buffalo cows lying dead, side by side. I jumped off my horse, cut out their tongues, tied them to my saddle, and took them home. Buffalo tongue was very choice.

There were many bands of hunters on the plains beside ours. In all my years of buffalo hunting, I never destroyed buffalo for their pelts alone. I always took the whole carcass, except the head, home.

My wife had once said that since we were going to make a living hunting buffalo, she did not want me to kill more than we could dry and pack. She told me that if I brought in an extra hide without the carcass, she would not dress it. One day my brother-in-law and I were travelling on the prairie, and we sighted a little herd of buffalo. I let fly and killed a cow. We skinned it, and took a little of the fattest part of the animal. When we reached our tent, I threw the hide and saddle down. My wife smiled, and lightly kicked the hide away. She meant what she said. I gave the hide to my mother-in-law.

On the second day that we were in camp, an Indian galloped up to see if we could let him have some cartridges. He told us that Pierre Quazanse and his woman had been shot by a Blackfoot band near the ravine where I had seen the objects. They belonged to another band of hunters, and while they were skinning buffalo the Indians had shot and cut them to pieces, and had drunk the blood out of their hearts. One Arrow said that it was well I had taken my horse's advice.

After the second day of this particular hunt there were a great many buffalo shot for their hides. Too many. But I can say that very few of the hunters in our brigade wanted to kill buffalo just for the hides.

We camped there for a week. We had a hundred people in our brigade, and they were all loaded—the carts followed the hunters. It took us four days to get home. All around us the buffalo travelled. When we got back to Round Plain, we found the buffalo there, too. We had a good time that winter. Plenty of buffalo.

The Yankees shot more buffalo for their hides than all the Indian and half-breed hunters put together. The Indians knew better. They did not want to see the buffalo gone forever. Parties of Yankees used to come up to the North-West to shoot for sport. They would sit on a hill and shoot. Once Buffalo Bill came on a shooting trip, and shot five hundred buffalo—just for fun.

Colonel Cody was known as "Buffalo Bill," because he contracted with the Kansas Pacific Railway to supply its laborers with buffalo meat. In eighteen months he killed four thousand two hundred and eighty buffalo. In 1883 he organized the "Wild West Show," an exhibition designed to represent life on the frontier.

In March a big blizzard came. It lasted for three days. Three miles from our place, a big band of buffalo that tried to cross the river fell through the ice and were frozen in. Toward spring, when it began to thaw, the Indians cut the ice, got the buffalo out, and saved the hides and carcasses. There were over a thousand buffalo frozen in the ice.

After that I spent my time trading with the Indians. I was on good terms with them, and most of them came to my house to trade. I felt sorry for them. The traders were charging ridiculous prices for their goods, and in return were giving the ignorant Indians poor prices for their furs.

Just about this time an Indian came to my house with five first quality robes. I asked him what he wanted for them. He replied that for four robes he would take two Hudson's Bay blankets, and for the other one he would take tea, sugar, tobacco, and ammunition.

I told him that the Indians always gave four buffalo robes for two blankets, but that I was going to cut my price and give him two Hudson's Bay blankets for three robes. I did this, and for the other two robes, I gave him tea, sugar, tobacco, and ammunition.

When we were through trading, I asked this Indian—he was a headman—if his band, and others, knew that the Indians had been paying far too much for everything. Then I picked up a stick of tobacco. I gave it to him, and told him to go back to his people, cut up this tobacco, invite the Chief and headmen to smoke, and tell them that if they would bring their furs to me—only good furs, of course—I would pay them a good price.

They came in crowds. This was One Arrow's band. They were fine hunters. They brought me the very best of furs, and were very greatly pleased with my cut-rates. In no time at all I had all my stuff sold out.

It paid me to cut my prices. It saved me the expense of outfitting dog-sleds and going out on the prairie. Dogs were expensive to buy and to feed, and there was always the danger of getting lost or frozen to death in blizzards. There were no marked highways in those days! There were only the old Hudson's Bay trails, and our trading trips took us far from these. Our only guide during the day was our sense of direction, and at night we used the stars. We set our course in the direction we wished to travel. When we camped in the snow, we set our sleds pointing toward our course.

I had traded all my goods before the other traders knew what I had done. Angry, they came and accused me of cutting prices and spoiling their trade. I told them that they had taken advantage of the Indians long enough, and that I intended giving them the prices their furs should bring.

That winter I got about a hundred and sixty buffalo robes, and about two hundred other furs—wolf, fox, badger, and similar small skins. We packed up and left Round Plain on the 25th of April, 1866. There were thirty families in the brigade.

When we got to Fort Garry, my brother-in-law—I always camped with him about three miles from the Fort—had a message for me. Two fur buyers had come from Saint Paul to meet the brigades from the plains. Having heard that I would have the best of furs, they left a message for me not to sell until I had seen them.

The next morning the buyers arrived. When they asked me if I had good furs, I told them that we might have different tastes. I might think they were good; they might think otherwise. The leading buyer agreed and asked to see them.

I directed my man to go to one of the carts and bring in two bundles. There were ten robes in each package. I cut the strings on one of the bundles, and asked the Yankee to shake the skins, to spread them out, to examine them properly. He did so. Then he asked if all the furs were as good as these. I told him to look for himself, and cut the string on the second bundle.

He wanted to know how many robes I had, and if they were all as good as these. I replied that I had a hundred and sixty-five buffalo robes that were as good or better than those I had shown him. You see, I hadn't shown him the best robes. He said that he hadn't intended buying that many, but if all my robes were like those he had seen he would like to have them all. I told myself that I had the fellow, and that he would pay me my price for these robes.

He wanted to know how much I would take for each of them. I asked him to make me an offer, since I wanted to sell, and he wanted to buy. If it were good, I would take it; if not, I wouldn't. He asked me how fifteen dollars apiece would suit me. I told him it didn't, that I wanted twenty. I saw that this man knew good furs, and that he would be willing to pay a good price for mine. He told his companion that the price was high, adding that the robes were good. He asked his partner if they had money enough.

They withdrew and talked together. The leading buyer came back and say, "Welsh, you have us cornered. We haven't got money enough, but if you will come down fifty cents on each robe, we can buy."

I told him that I had set my price and must get it. I had noticed that he was wearing a fine watch and chain. There wasn't much difference I told him, only about eighty dollars, and, if he were short of money, I would take his watch and chain. He said he hated to part with his watch, but I told him that sometimes we had to make sacrifices and that I was offering him a fine price for his watch. He agreed, after telling me that I was a hard dealer. That gave me just twenty dollars apiece for my buffalo robes. He paid me in bills, thirty-three hundred dollars. I sold my other furs for a thousand dollars. I now had forty-three hundred dollars in cash and a good watch.

I told my brother-in-law that I would be happy to make him a present of the watch, because I did not know how to use it. Later I met the Yankees again, when they were through buying. They told me they had bought over five thousand dollars worth of furs, but that mine were the best.

Chapter Six

A Giving Away Dance

The first year that I wintered at Round Plain, after I was married—the winter of 1865—I attended a Giving Away Dance. This is a real Indian dance. In the old days on the plains, the buffalo hunters and traders were expected to take part in these dances. We were all wintering together in Indian Territory, and were surrounded by Indian lodges. The Indians were our customers and we had to be sociable.

The Indian law was that an Indian could never lend his horse, his wife, or his gun. A horse and a gun therefore were the most valuable presents that one could give to an Indian.

The name of the Chief who sponsored this Giving Away Dance was Moon-e-ash, which means "White Man." He was a brother of Chief One Arrow (Kah-payuk-wah-skoonum) one of the signers of the *Forts Carlton and Pitt* treaty.[1] Moon-e-ash was very tall, and he had fair hair and blue eyes. He invited me and some of the other people from the winter brigades to go to his lodge.

When we got there, he told us that he wanted to have a Giving Away Dance. We told him to please himself, that we supposed he knew what he was doing, and if he wanted us to do anything we would.

He had quite a number of people in his lodge, and there were more outside. He called for them to assemble. The Indians came. Altogether there must have been thirty or forty

---

1. Moon-e-ash: Probably Moon-oo-yahs. He signed the Fort Carlton Treaty on Aug. 28, 1876.

men in the lodge, Indians and half-breeds. Moon-e-ash told the crowd that he was going to begin the dance, and that it would last for five days and five nights.

Then he told one of his men to load the five guns that were lying on the floor of the lodge. The headman loaded the guns and laid them down. Then Moon-e-ash ordered his wife to bring the marrow fat that had been prepared for the dance. This was marrow fat mixed with crushed dried choke cherries and packed into a bladder. It looked good and tasted good. It was served on a very clean dish.

Moon-e-ash told his guests that he wanted them all to make the dance a success, to take it seriously, to pray with him to the Manitou. He beat the drum, as he began to dance and sing to the Manitou. Everyone joined in. Then Moon-e-ash said, "Now I'm ready. How! Now my men, five men take one gun each."

The men went outside and fired off the guns. Moon-e-ash sang again. When he had finished the song, he thanked his listeners and told them that the shooting off of the guns was an answer, or promise, from the Manitou that the dance would be a success. If only four of the guns had gone off it would have signified the Manitou's permission for only four days of dancing.

Moon-e-ash said, "Thank you, thank you. You have listened to me, to my skeleton."

Moon-e-ash now ordered the marrow fat to be opened. He took the dish and, holding it with both hands, he took a bite off the fat. Then he passed the dish to his neighbor. Each one took a bite off the fat as it was passed around, and the dish came back to Moon-e-ash. It was time now for Moon-e-ash to dance. He told me that I would have to give him a present. I gave him a box of figs. After he received the present he sang again.

> *On-dee-ah-o-ma-kak-we-a-ya-e-yen.* (Repeat 3 times.)
> (Translation: Now, my friends, this is what I am giving you.)
> *Yayayaya yayaya yayayaya yayaya, ha–a!!* (Repeat 3 times.)

Moon-e-ash gave me a fine buffalo robe.

On the second night of the Giving Away Dance, we heard a knock on the parchment door of our house. It sounded like a drum. I asked who was there. My wife's uncle, André Trottier, answered and asked my wife to get up at once. She did. We opened the door. Trottier handed my wife seven long shaggannappis (long ropes of buffalo hide) and told her to dance. My wife said that she could not dance. Trottier answered that if she did not dance she would not get her present. I went to the parchment door and beat the time upon it. My wife danced.

Trottier and I sang:

> *Cha-mak-pa-cah-qua-ne-na-tah.* (Repeat 3 times.)
> *Yayayaya yayaya yayayaya yayaya, ha–a!*
> *yayayaya yayaya yayayaya yayaya, ha–a!*
> *yayayaya yayaya yayayaya yayaya, ha–a!*
> (Translation: I hope that we will live long.)

Then Trottier told my wife to come and get her present. There were seven horses at the ends of the seven shaggannappis, five buffalo robes, two bags of pemmican, and two bales of dried meat.

Trottier sang:

> *Ke-ne-wash-ka-we-pe-maw-te-she-non.*
> (This is a very fast horse that I am giving you.)
> *yayayaya yayaya yayayaya yayaya, ha–a!*
> *yayayaya yayaya yayayaya yayaya, ha–a!*
> *yayayaya yayaya yayayaya yayaya, ha–a!*
> *Ah-du-a-me-cah-we-ke-wa-tu.*
> *Ah-wah-ka-me-e-tan.*
> (I'm giving you the reins now.)
> *yayayaya yayaya yayayaya yayaya, ha–a!*
> *yayayaya yayaya yayayaya yayaya, ha–a!*
> *yayayaya yayaya yayayaya yayaya, ha–a!*

I was so surprised that I didn't know what to do about all these presents. I had never been to a Giving Away Dance before. It happened that, at this time, there was a priest visiting in the settlement. Next morning, I went to his camp, told him that Trottier had given us all those presents, and asked what I should do.

He explained that the whole settlement had to take part in the dance, and each one was expected to contribute. He said, "My dear man, you are a trader. The horses you will know what to do with. But the dried meat, pemmican, and buffalo robes—estimate how much they are worth and give Trottier as much as if you were buying them from him. About the horses you can please yourself."

Well, we had a very fine cart that Trottier's wife was always wishing for. We gave her that, first making her dance for it. I gave the cart for one horse, and for the other six horses, I gave Trottier six of mine. For the dried meat, and buffalo robes, I gave him a sixty pound case of tea, then plugs of T & B tobacco, and twenty pounds of sugar.

The dance kept on for five days. I went only one day. I got presents from other men also. Moses Landry made me dance. He poked a shagannappi through the door of my tent. On the end of the line was a horse that I had tried to buy from him several times, but had not been able to get at any price for it was his favorite horse.

I had a good buffalo horse, a good racer, that could run a mile in two minutes. I called him "Big Knee" because he had a lump on his knee. This lump did not affect him in any way. Big Knee was worth three hundred dollars.

The next night, the fourth night of the dance, I took Big Knee with me, and also a brand new rifle, into which I put fourteen cartridges. Then I went to Landry's house, and knocked on his parchment door. I asked him if he were there, and fired the fourteen shots in the air. This was to notify him that I had come to give him something. I made him dance and sing. I gave him Big Knee and the rifle.

Next morning before breakfast, Landry came to my house with another shagannappi and two buffalo robes. He made me dance and sing for them. Well, that's the way the Giving Away Dance went on until the five days had expired. At the end of the five days, Moon-e-ash sang his song and the dance was over.

One day, in my fifth year at Round Plain, I was sitting in the house alone. By and by an Indian came in and asked if this was Wa-ka-kootchick's house. When I replied that it was and asked him what he wanted, he told me that he had a message for me from his Chief, Shash-apew.

Then he told me that he supposed I knew that his band had a dancing tent at Red Deer Lake. I replied that I did, and asked him his name. It was Pish-e-quat (Blackguard) he told me. He had been sent by Shash-apew, he said, to warn the half-breeds not to hunt buffalo in his territory unless they were willing to pay a duty on every buffalo they killed. There were lots of buffalo, he said, and we could kill all we wanted, provided that we came to Shash-apew's terms.

I told him that Shash-apew must think he was God. Then I explained to him that God had not put those buffalo in the world for Shash-apew to be the boss of them all. They were to be for all the people. I would promise to pay Shash-apew a duty on the buffalo, I told him, if he would deliver them.

Then I went on to explain that when we sold a horse to an Indian we put a shaggannappi on the neck of the horse, put the end of the shaggannappi in the hand of the Indian, and by doing so, the horse was his.

I told him that our brigade would be at his camp in three days, and when we got there we would want about one hundred and fifty buffalo. If they would bring us that many, each with a shaggannappi on its neck, we would, I promised, pay a duty on every one.

Pish-e-quat said that I knew it would be impossible for them to do that, and accused me of trying to hold his band up. I asked him why he wanted us to pay for buffalo then, since he couldn't deliver them. He answered that the headmen of his band believed that the Indians were more entitled to the buffalo than the white men. I assured him that the buffalo belonged to whoever could shoot them.

The other traders in the brigade were away, so I decided

to send Shash-apew a message on my own. I got some tea, sugar, and half a fathom of tobacco, which was equal to one yard. This Hudson's Bay tobacco was twisted like a rope, and sold by the fathom. It was the finest tobacco made. I gave these presents to Pish-e-quat. I told him to take them back to the dancing tent to Shash-apew, and to tell him exactly what I had said. He was to say also that, if the Indians disturbed us when we went to hunt, they would get into trouble.

The brigade started for Red Deer Lake. At the end of the second day we reached Shash-apew's camp. There were about fifty tents in the encampment. Between two and three hundred Crees had assembled here for the dancing. As far as we could see, the buffalo grazed, or stood in big herds. We camped beside the Chief's dancing tent.

The dancing tent was huge. It held about two hundred dancers. It was formed by combining the buffalo-skin coverings of several other lodges, and covered over an acre of ground.

After supper a message came to us from Shash-apew (Spread Sitter)—he called himself my uncle—inviting us to the dancing tent. Trottier, the elder Dumont, and myself were the three principal men in the brigade. We went to the dancing tent.

My uncle, Shash-apew, thanked me for the tea, sugar, and tobacco which I had sent. He thanked me also for my message. He said we could go and shoot as many buffalo as we liked, that there would be no trouble.

The next morning we got on our buffalo runners—we had twenty of these buffalo horses—and chased the buffalo. It was a good race. After supper Charles Trottier counted the buffalo we had brought into camp. We had killed, skinned, and brought to camp a hundred and twenty-five buffalo.

Next day we made another run. We killed just as many. In two days we had killed two hundred and fifty buffalo, skinned, and cut them up ready to pack in our carts. We packed our meat and went back to our camping ground. We heard no more from this blackguard about his "duty."

CHAPTER SEVEN

A Hunter's Handicap

lthough on friendly terms with the white men, the Cree and the Blackfoot tribes still fought bitterly and raided each other's territory. There lived on the Saskatchewan River at this time two young Cree warriors—brothers—named Mi-cou-chusta-con (Red Hair), and Shaw-wish-ti-con (Yellow Hair). One had very red hair, the other had yellow hair, and they both had very white skin. They were pure blooded Crees.

Yellow Hair, the youngest, and another brave, Pasqua-ka-tick (Bare Forehead), decided to make a raid on the Blackfoot tribe. On a flat at the forks of the Red Deer River, near where Calgary is to-day, there was a big Blackfoot encampment of about four hundred tents. Here there was feasting and dancing in celebration of a recent war victory. They had, a few days earlier, thinned out a tribe called the little Sioux, or known in Sioux as Pooka-Looka.

Yellow Hair and his braves stole away from camp one night and set out for the Blackfoot camp. They spent several nights spying on the movements of their enemies. After many nights of feasting and dancing, the Blackfoot warriors slept. Yellow Hair decided to act. Before daylight one morning he and his man entered the first tent they came to. In the tent a Blackfoot and his wife slept. The Crees drove their long, sharp butcher knives into the hearts of their victims. They took their scalps. Then they stole fifty horses and took them to their encampment on the Round Plain, a place called long ago,

Wapoose-ah-wak-can-mista-hay-tchick. This meant in Cree, "the place where there are lots of rabbits." It is about thirty-five miles from Calgary on the south side of the Saskatchewan River.

After this successful raid, fifty horses and two scalps, Yellow Hair and his brave held a scalp dance. But first they had to fix the scalps. To tan a scalp, the Indians stretched it over four little sticks. When it was dry, they took it off this frame. Then they got a little pole about the size of my fist, and seven or eight feet long, and tied the scalp to the end of it. A little cross-piece kept the scalp stretched. On the skin side of the scalp, they painted in colors the face and body of a person. They painted the pole also with vermilion. Then they held a big pow-wow. Indians and half-breeds were invited to feast and dance in the great dance tent.

While they were dancing, Red Hair, jealous of his brother's success, told another brave that he, too, had decided to take to the war-path. He argued that his brother, who was only a child, had taken fifty horses and two scalps, what would happen if he took a party? Sixty braves agreed to go with him. He was the sixty-first.

They started and followed the south branch of the Saskatchewan River until they were opposite what is now Medicine Hat. Red Hair told his band there must be a band of Blackfoot Indians near this point. They decided to camp there, kill buffalo, dry meat, and prepare for war.

Red Hair sent Pointed Cap, who was with the party, and another Indian to scout around and find out how far away the Blackfoot camp was. They went. It was still in the same place, and the Blackfoot warriors were preparing for a raid on an enemy camp.

When the scouts reported this to Red Hair, he told them to put up a tent for him. He wanted to consult with the Manitou to learn, among other things, how successful his raid would be.

The braves prepared the tent. They made it out of their clothes and blankets, and lashed it properly. Then they bound around his neck, and then lashed his entire body. The thongs were placed about an inch apart all up and down his body, front and back. Finally they threw him into his tent to talk to his Manitou. He began to sing his war song.

As he sang, he crawled out of his shaggannappi, out of his lashing, without breaking a knot. He shed it as a snake sheds his skin. That proved to the Indians the power of the Manitou. Then he told his men that it was no good, they would not succeed, but he intended to raid the Blackfoot camp anyway. Those who wanted to follow him could, while those who did not wish to, could return to the band.

All of the men in the band were fond of Red Hair, so they decided to follow him. On his scouting trip, Pointed Cap had come upon a Blackfoot tent, entered it, killed the Indian, and taken the Blackfoot woman for his wife. I saw this Blackfoot often in the Cree camp. The Blackfoot camp was aware of the Crees, and the warriors were waiting for them to come.

In the attack on the first tent, Red Hair led the others. A Blackfoot shot him dead as he lifted the flap to enter. The two tribes fought for quite a while. But the Blackfoot tribe was prepared, and, besides, they were on horseback while the Crees were on foot.

The Blackfoot tribe won. They shot all the Crees but two. These two, although terribly wounded, got away in the bush and escaped. They managed to crawl to the river, where they got some big sticks, tied them together to make a raft, and floated down the south branch of the Saskatchewan River to Round Plain.

I often saw the survivors of that fight. The Indians called it Red Hair's big fight. These Indians were badly cut up and scarred, but the Blackfoot woman in One Arrow's band dressed their wounds, nursed them, and they soon got all right again.

I had one very hard buffalo hunt that year. I had a very sore hand. It was all swollen up and blood poisoning had set in. The buffalo had drifted toward the west, and I couldn't get a boy or man to help me. Every man was out for himself. But we had a girl working for us, and, of course, there was my wife.

My wife and the girl said they would help me, so we started with other members of the brigade. I had my hand in a sling. On the second day, about one hundred miles south-west, we came on a big herd of buffalo. I asked my wife to saddle my racer and give me my gun. She protested that I would not be able to kill buffalo, but I said that I could do something with my right hand. It was my left that was crippled.

Altogether there were about thirty hunters in the brigade. When we got close to the buffalo, Anthony Trottier gave the word to go. I let my bridle fall on my hunter's neck. A trained buffalo horse knew that this was always intended as the signal to go.

I threw myself forward, pulled my sore hand out of the sling and my gun out of the gun-coat. Holding my gun in my right hand, I ran my horse right in amongst the buffalo. I scattered the herd out a little, ran my horse against two fat buffalo cows, laid my gun across my sore arm, and shot and killed the two cows. Then I stopped. The other hunters went on.

My wife came up with the other carts. She unhitched her horses from the cart, and I tied my racer to it. I took my knife—my wife had sharpened it properly—and, with my right hand, caught one cow by the right horn and threw her over on her back. Still holding the horn, I twisted the neck and put the head under the shoulder. That made it solid. It was now ready to skin. I fixed both cows the same way, solid, so they wouldn't tip over.

Now I took my knife and ripped the hide from the throat right down the belly to the tail. Then I ripped the hide on the legs from the hoof right up the leg. I stripped the skin off the front of the cow, then I turned it over again and skinned the back, keeping the hide under the cow all the time to prevent the meat from getting dirty.

That was the first stage in skinning buffalo. Now I took my knife and ran it through the animal's carcass from the head to the tail. I spread this meat out. Next I removed the tripe, then the heart, the fat, the kidneys, and laid them all aside.

Then I cut the other side of the animal, removed the ribs, stretched the carcass out, cut the tongue out of the head, and cut the head off and threw it on one side. I next cut off the neck. After that I cut the backbone through just where the hips join, and laid that aside as good meat. Then I took the rump and split it into two parts. That was also put aside as good meat.

As I worked, my sore hand became supple. I could not help using it. In no time I had the two cows skinned and cut up. These cows were almost as fat as pigs. One had two fingers of fat, and the other three fingers.

The pain in my hand that night was terrible. I couldn't sleep. I had to hold my hand up all night. The next morning there was a bigger band of buffalo than the day before. We were camped right in the path of the buffalo. They were travelling in large herds, and there were anywhere from a thousand upward in a herd.

My wife did not want me to chase buffalo when I was suffering so with my hand. But I told her to have the girl bring my gun, my horse, and my saddle, and help me on my runner; I would do the rest. I mounted my runner and away I went with the riders—just as many riders as the day before.

I was the first in among the buffalo. I shot five, but they were not as good as those I had shot the day before. They were just average. I didn't pick them. My wife and the girl drove up with two carts. My hand had stopped paining. I threw off my vest, turned up my sleeves, and skinned and cut up the buffalo.

Night came. How I suffered! My hand was swollen to more than twice its size. An old half-breed doctor, Louis Landry—Ch-bu-toon, which meant "Shoe Button" or "Vest Button"—came and examined my hand. We were no relation, but he called me his grandchild. He told me that it would fester and break out in eight or nine days, and then it would be all right. I kept soaking it in hot water, and bathing it with alcohol, or liniment.

He told me that he could cure me but that I must rest, and

I must stop chasing buffalo. I told him that I could not stop running buffalo. I must take my part, with all the other people who were killing buffalo and getting rich. I never gave up. I raced after the buffalo with the others, with that terrible pain constantly in my hand, and at night no sleep. With only my wife and the hired girl to help me, I cut up and brought back to camp all the meat of the fifty cows I shot. At the end of the ninth day the hand broke. The sinews had rotted. The old half-breed doctor pulled them out.

Never in all my buffalo chasing did I get hurt by buffalo, nor do I know of any other hunters that were ever attacked by buffalo. In the race, the buffalo were too frightened to stop for fight. Sometimes a wounded buffalo would make a dash at me, but I would let fly and knock him down. A man had to be quick with his gun.

A good buffalo horse knows a lot. He knows what he is about. Always when I got on my buffalo runner, he started to lope, to dance, he was so glad to run—le-gallon. If I did not start right away, he would tremble with excitement.

There is another reason why we never got hurt. Always before starting on a buffalo hunt, the hunters in my brigade got on their knees and said a little prayer.

We liked to shoot buffalo cows because they had the best meat, the fattest and tenderest, and in the fall and winter they had the best hides. The two-year-old animals had fine hides. We shot these in June and July when they were fat and profitable for pemmican. The hides of the old buffalo were poor. The hair was too coarse. In the fall we shot nothing but cows. They were fine for pemmican and dried meat. We were very particular about choosing our animals. That was our business.

In the spring of 1868 we went back to Fort Garry. I sold my buffalo robes, badger, wolf, skunk, and so on. In all I got five thousand dollars for my furs. Each man in the brigade had his own business. We carried gold or paper money. Sometimes we had a red cotton handkerchief full of bills. I often thought of putting money in the bank, but always I waited for a bigger haul. I was becoming a more important trader all the time.

I started out again that same year with an outfit of two thousand dollars. Always up to this time I had been using Red River carts, but now I was making money, and I was feeling proud.

I went to James MacKay, at St. James, a parish near Fort Garry, and bought ten carts from him. They were Red River carts, but had been made in the States, in Saint Paul, in the style of a waggon. They had only two wheels, but were lighter, stronger, and looked neater than the old Red River carts that I had been using.

I asked MacKay what he would take for ten of these carts. He told me that they were worth fifty dollars apiece, but he did not want to sell them because he had bought them to use himself. He was a trader, mail-carrier, and business man. I told him that fifty dollars might be all right for one cart, but that I wanted them wholesale, and asked how much he would take for ten. He asked me if I would pay cash. Then he asked me how forty dollars apiece would be. I told him that I would take the carts, and counted out the cash, four hundred dollars, and asked him to bring them.

He told me that I was the right kind of man to deal with, adding that the barefoot boy was getting on. In Saint James they used to call me the barefoot boy.

I sold my old carts to other traders for what I could get—five, ten, or fifteen dollars apiece. Now I had a fine new outfit. It was greatly admired by the other traders. I made up my mind to make, through the winter, a whole new set of harnesses, so I went to a harness-maker and bought bridles, straps, back-straps, and a lot of buckles.

It was after freeze-up when we reached Round Plain. After unpacking and fixing things up, we crossed the Saskatchewan River on a buffalo-hunt. The buffalo were beginning to get scarce. We did not get many, and unfortunately, those were about all the buffalo we got all winter. The *big* herds had disappeared. The Indians almost starved that winter. We were all right, because we had, on reaching Round Plain, bought a lot of provisions for the winter from the various traders—pemmican, dried meat, and fat. As the winter progressed, we sold a good deal of it back to them.

I saw one trader there—but first I must explain what a pemmican bag is like and how pemmican is prepared. We took a buffalo hide and stretched it out properly, then ripped it in the centre to make four pieces out of it. Then we took one piece and doubled it evenly. We cut this piece a little round at the corners, and sewed the two bottom corners with sinew. The top was left open. Then we packed the bag half-full of pemmican, pounding it down with a wooden mallet, adding more pemmican, and pounding that down until the bag was full. I could guess fairly well when there were a hundred pounds in the bag. When the bag was full, we lapped it over at the top and cut the corners round. Then we took a needle full of sinew and sewed it up. The bag was now thrown on the ground, flattened with a mallet and made into a nice shape, not too fat, not too thin. If you want to eat something that will stay with you eat pemmican. A pemmican bag held about a hundred pounds, and was three feet long, and solid when packed.

I should explain how the pemmican was prepared. I took a big Hudson's Bay copper kettle that held about ten gallons. I mixed that full of tallow and fat. I melted it over a fire. I let it boil. Then onto a buffalo hide I spread the cut-up dried buffalo meat which had been pounded into shreds or flakes with a flail. Next I took a small kettle, and out of the large kettle of boiling fat I dipped and poured the boiling fat over the buffalo meat, and mixed it properly, using a shovel. It took two people to make pemmican, one to pour, one to mix.

This trader, his name was Antoine La Rocque, and he was a half-breed, took a pemmican bag that weighed less than a hundred pounds, perhaps ninety-two pounds or something like that, and cut it into three pieces. He sold one of these pieces to an Indian for a horse that was worth fifty dollars. he got three horses for those three pieces of pemmican. That man got to be very rich. I saw him one spring—we went together to Fort Garry—sell ten thousand dollars worth of furs. Then he lost all of his money. The year of the Rebellion I had to lend him money. He was down to one horse and wanted to buy another to make a team so that he could draw freight to make a little money to feed his family. I lent him two hundred dollars. He was to pay me in two years at eight per cent. I got the principal but no interest.

That winter the Indians rode away in all directions, wherever they heard there was buffalo. The old Indians were great story-tellers, and when I wasn't busy I used to visit in their camps and listen to their war stories. There were many stories told too about the old Hudson's Bay posts. One of the men who had worked at Fort Edmonton told me about the death of John Rowand,[1] Chief Hudson's Bay Factor of that post.

Rowand was before my time, but he was one of the principal factors of his day in this country. I knew his son well. I had worked for him for four years at what is now Silver Heights, Winnipeg, when I was a boy. John Rowand was a very

1. John Rowand built Fort Edmonton for the Hudson's Bay Company in 1795. He was still Chief Factor there as late as 1840. Fort Edmonton was at that time one of the most important posts of the Company, west of Fort Garry.

The Hudson's Bay Company records show that John Rowand dropped dead at Fort Pitt on the 30th of May, 1854. He was paying a visit to his son. And, a letter from Sir George Simpson to Alexander Rowand, dated 29th July, 1856, relates the story of the proposed transfer of John Rowand's remains to the city of his birth-place. It does not say if they finally arrived.

"It was one of the last instructions your father gave John, on the day preceding his death, that his bones were not to be left in the Indian country but removed to Canada and interred near those of his own father. I accordingly directed that the body should be disinterred last winter and brought out to Norway House, from whence I conveyed it this summer in my own canoe to Red River, but some of the crew having discovered the contents of the package, I was afraid they might (from a superstitious feeling) drop it overboard at some time, and therefore had it repacked and sent to York Factory for transmission to England by the ship, from whence it will be forwarded to this place (Lachine). The wish of the family at Red River is to erect a handsome monument to their father's memory in Montreal by subscription among themselves and I have undertaken to see the design carried out . . . The cost of the monument I placed over the grave of my poor wife was $500, and I think for that sum I could now get a very handsome tomb erected for the reception of your father's bones . . . "

wicked man, hasty, quick-tempered. His son, John, was always fighting with the hired men of the Company, and one day he got into a bad fight and was getting the worst of it. One of the employees ran into his father's office and told the old man about it. The old man came running out, threw up his hands, shouted to his son, "Can't you do better than that?" and fell dead.

It seems that the old factor had always expressed a wish that his bones should be buried in Canada. Rowand was a big man. He weighed about three hundred pounds. However, his wife and sons decided to have the bones sent to Canada by way of England.

They called in an old Indian named Ka-min-a-coush, told him to cut the body to pieces and boil the bones. They gave this old Indian three horses and five gallons of Hudson's Bay rum to attend to this work. So the old Indian drank his glass of rum, sharpened his knife properly, and cut the old factor to pieces, taking all of the bones out of his flesh. The men at the Post made a coffin, put the flesh into it, and buried the coffin at Fort Edmonton, just beside the old Fort.

Then Ka-min-a-coush got two big Hudson's Bay copper kettles, put the bones into them, added a lot of lye, and boiled them until there was nothing left, no flesh or sinew, just bare white bone. When they were done, the whole family gathered, and had the bones placed in a coffin. Then they shipped the coffin to the Chief Factor at Norway House, who placed it in a York Boat, which took it to York Factory where it was placed on board a boat bound for England. After leaving port a great storm arose which lasted for five days. The crew came to the conclusion that John Rowand's spirit was haunting them. He had been a tyrant in life. He was still master in death. They decided to take his bones and pitch them into the sea. This done, the storm died down.

I did not have more than seventy-five robes to take back to Fort Garry that spring. Furs were no price at all. But I had some other stuff. I just covered expenses. I did not make a cent of profit, but I had some goods left.

When I took account of stock, I could not, of course, put it down in writing. So this is what I did. I would figure up how much goods I had taken out, and how many dollars worth. Then I would estimate how much I had sold, and how much I had left. That year I had seventy-five robes. They would bring me, I figured, at least a thousand dollars. Some other furs should bring me say about five hundred dollars. I always reckoned the stuff I had to sell lower than the price at which I sold. Then I'd balance the two things together. I've got so much goods, and I've got so many furs; I'm not in the hole yet.

CHAPTER EIGHT

The Blackfoot Fight the Crees

I tackled the seventh year without such a big outfit. Still I had fully two thousand dollars worth of goods. The brigade kept going to Round Plain because it was a lucky place. The buffalo used to winter and travel there more than at any other place on the plains. It was near water and was a fine wintering ground. It was sheltered on the north, and open on the south.

We had a good hunt and came back to the wintering grounds. All the hunters came back well loaded, but, aside from that hunt, we didn't have much luck that winter. The buffalo had gone south again. Very few were seen on the plains. I had a poor winter as far as business went.

About this time the Indians talked a good deal about the beginning and end of an Indian tribe called Oosh-ka-chee-mush-shak (Little Dogs) which had been wiped out by a dose of smallpox. The Little Dogs were a mixed tribe, Crees, Salteaux, Assiniboines, and Stoneys. They lived at the Broken Shell Butte, so-called because there were lots of shells there, a little south of Wood Mountain.

Finally these Indians drank so much alcohol that it made them insane. They had been drinking for a long time when they began to fight among themselves and to butcher each other like dogs. The fighting started about the beginning of March, and continued until the middle of April. There were about a thousand Indians in the encampment, and almost all of them got smallpox. Those who were not sick still fought. When the camp recovered from the smallpox, there were only seven lodges of these Indians left, about eighty or ninety in all.

When spring opened out in May, they travelled toward the south branch of the Saskatchewan River. In June they crossed the south branch of the Saskatchewan River and came to a place that in the early days was called The Basin Lake. This place is now called Rosetown.

These Indians still fought as they travelled, and killed each other at every chance. They had a very old woman with them that they treated as a slave. When they reached The Basin Lake, they camped there for a time.

One clear bright day it began to thunder and lighten, and soon it rained. By and by it rained fire. The Indians threw themselves into the lake to get cooled off. Instead of getting cool they got hotter. They were all burned to death except a few and the old woman, their slave, who lived to tell the tale. Other tribes reported this story also.

The Indian who told me this story was Ne-ooka-shick, Four Sky. He was there himself. I asked him what he thought caused the band to be wiped out. He replied in Cree that it was A-moi-ya-pa-me-coo-e-chick, which meant that it was a punishment from the great Manitou. That was the Indians' belief.[1]

The Cree Indians were great hunters. When there was no hunting they kept themselves amused by holding dancing parties, or going on the war-path. The Blackfoot tribe was their hated enemy, and they fought them every chance they got.

This is how an Indian Chief invited his Indians to go on the war-path. He took a fine new red Hudsons' Bay blanket, and a fathom of red Hudson's Bay cloth (two yards), covered his horse with them, wrapped a black blanket around his

1. Four Sky belonged to Piapot's Reserve. He came to see me two years ago and I cross-questioned him about this story. He repeated it exactly as he first told it to me on the plains many years ago. Word for word. A smart man, Four Sky. He had two wives.

The time of this plague was around 1851, as the Indians figured. It carried off Alexander Goulet, a trader, too. A good man.

body, and led the horse around the camp singing his war song. That was his invitation to his braves to follow him.

Cree War Cry

Ya-ya-ya-ya, ya-ya-ya-ya, ya-ya-ya-ya, hi, how!
Ya-ya-ya-ya, ya-ya-ya-ya, ya-ya-ya-ya, hi, how!
We-wa-koo-mah-ka-ye-mick.
We-wa-koo-mah-ka-ye-mick.
Ya-ya-ya-ya, ya-ya-ya-ya, ya-ya-ya-ya, hi, how!
Ya-ya-ya-ya, ya-ya-ya-ya, ya-ya-ya-ya, hi, how!
(Translation: Have mercy on me, my friends, have mercy on me. I'm going on a war party. I want all my friends that want to join me to come.)

Ya-ya-ya-ya, ya-ya-ya-ya, ya-ya-ya-ya, hi, how!
Ya-ya-ya-ya, ya-ya-ya-ya, ya-ya-ya-ya, hi, how!
Oh-mah-ki-ye-too-ye.
She-pee-ah-ne-ta-ne-we
She-pa-wa-ta-yan.
Ya-ya-ya-ya, ya-ya-ya-ya, ya-ya-ya-ya, hi, how!
Ya-ya-ya-ya, ya-ya-ya-ya, ya-ya-ya-ya, hi, how!
(Translation: I'm going to the forks of the Red Deer and the Saskatchewan Rivers. I am going to war with the Blackfoot tribe.)

Pointed Cap assembled about eighty-five choice warriors to make ready to travel to the forks of the Red Deer River and the Saskatchewan to make war on the Blackfoot Indians. This Pointed Cap was not a chief, but headman of a big tribe of Crees who had an encampment near Edmonton. They went off, and, as usual, a day from the fighting ground they stopped and made provisions for several days. They killed buffalo and got everything ready. Pointed Cap sent two of his warriors out to scout to find out how far they were from the big Blackfoot camp. He told them to take their time, but that if they were not back by the end of the fourth day, he would think that something had happened to them.

The scouts returned at the end of the third day, and reported that they had found a big Blackfoot encampment of one hundred tents. Pointed Cap said that they would conquer them easily, that that would be about one tent apiece for each of his men. Next morning they started. They camped within five miles of the Blackfoot encampment, where they could see all of the tents and horses.

These Crees did not attack in open fight, but crept upon the Blackfoot camp unawares. They started their raid at break of day, and pulled all the tents down but one. Father Lacombe was in that tent. He called out to the Crees to have mercy on the Blackfoot tribe, whom they had taken unawares. One Cree Indian shouted to Father Lacombe that if he put his head out of the tent he would blow his brains out.

Tying Knot said that Father Lacombe could not stop them. They killed men, women, and children, in all about five hundred. They completely destroyed that great camp. They took scalps, horses, and even lodges with them, and returned to their camp at Edmonton. They did not touch Father Lacombe. Years afterwards when Tying Knot became blind, he told me that his blindness was a punishment from God. He had meanwhile become a Christian. He had been too cruel, he thought, to the Indians whom he had killed. He had tortured them terribly. Father Lacombe reported that in this particular battle the Indians had fought like dogs, tearing and eating each other up.

Tying Knot was a great warrior. He belonged to the File Hills—Starblanket's band, and was one of the signers of the Qu'Appelle treaty. I knew this man on the plains and for forty years afterward. He died on the File Hills Reserve about sixteen years ago. He was very savage in his day. He told me a great many stories about his raids on the Blackfoot tribe. I am going to tell you a story he told me not long before he died.

It seems that once he was camped at a lake which the traders called Lac-le-Bœuf—Buffalo Lake, south of Edmonton. One day he told his braves that he had made up his mind to go on a war-party. They made preparations, and, in two or three days, started towards the big Blackfoot camp at the forks of the Red Deer. It was winter and there was snow on the ground. When they got there, Tying Knot said to his braves, "I begin to feel something. I think there are war parties around us. We had better get provisions and prepare for war."

They stopped, killed a fat buffalo cow and made enough pemmican to fill their grub sacks. They camped out in the open. They had no tents. Of course they could not carry tents when they went on the war-path. All they had with them were the provisions and the clothes they wore. Although the Indians were beginning at this time to buy and wear white men's clothes, they always wore Indian clothes when they went to war. These clothes were made out of buffalo skins tanned as soft as a glove. A properly tanned skin could be tied in a big red handkerchief. I seldom saw an Indian cold. Indians are hot-blooded.

When an Indian went on the war-path, he tied one of these finely tanned buffalo skins, or a Hudson's Bay blanket, around his neck, and strapped it lightly around his waist, so that he could throw it down if attacked. I found that many of the warriors preferred the Hudson's Bay blankets, for they were so warm and light. I had a great trade in these blankets. I want to say this, too, that the Hudson's Bay blankets are just as good to-day as they were when I sold them in trade. I used to buy the very best Hudson's Bay blankets at five dollars a pair, wholesale. Some of the Indians made blanket caps out of these blankets. They were called Capuchon.

To return to Tying Knot.[2] He and his brother started out to scout. They were two big men. Each one could run like a horse. They could out-run a horse in no time. Half a day's run from their camp, they saw a tent, and made for it.

They found a Blackfoot and his wife. Of course, they killed the Indian first, stabbed him and cut him open. Then they decided to take the woman alive. She resisted. Tying Knot was a powerful Indian. He caught hold of the woman to

2. "Tying Knot originally belonged to Big Bear's band. He travelled all over the country before he made treaty. After Treaty, Tying Knot came under Little Black Bear's Band. He was a headman. Black Bear's band traded with Alexander Henry at Rocky Mountain House, 1810–1811." See page 654, Henry's Journal—Elliot Coues, Editor.

drag her home. She fought like a tiger. She attacked him and knocked him down. He called his brother. They both took hold of her. For a few seconds it looked as though she was going to get the best of them both. Tying Knot said, "We can't take her alive to our camp, so we'll take her dead."

Tying Knot told his brother to catch her by the hair of the head and twist her neck, and that he would cut her throat. So they did. Then they cut her head off.

Pointed Cap (Chee-poo-astotin) roamed the Saskatchewan and Alberta country. That was about seventy-five years ago. He was a sly horse thief. Although a powerful warrior, he was a sort of outcast in his own tribe because of his mischief amongst other Indian tribes. He could speak several languages.

Finally, he decided to take a wife and live in his own camp. He intended to give up his old tricks. So, according to the Indian custom, he went to a creek from which the Indian girls got water, and began to ask each one for a drink. The one who gave him a drink would become his betrothed, and they would get married immediately. But Pointed Cap was not as lucky as he expected. Not one of the girls would give him a drink. He was extremely disappointed. But there was a very young girl with the others. Pointed Cap said to her, "You will give me a drink." She did. The other girls scolded her. They ran to camp and reported that this very young girl had given a drink to the celebrated warrior, Pointed Cap.

"Oh," said the Chief, "that is no disgrace. Pointed Cap can take care of, and provide for, her till she becomes old enough to marry by the Indian custom of giving a horse or a gun to her nearest relation." Now the Chief ordered a tepee put up and declared Pointed Cap to be married to this child. But he warned him at the same time that in occupying this tepee he was only accepting the girl as his future wife. Pointed Cap agreed to this.

As time went on, Pointed Cap did all he could to keep the little girl contented. But this did not last long. The child grew sick and died. The future husband was a widower. Pointed

Cap took the child's death very hard. He would walk a long distance from the camp and cry like a child. He lived in such gloom that everyone in the camp was sad. Of course he was only observing the Indian custom of mourning.

At last, one night while he was walking around moaning as usual, two young friends spoke to him about his grief. Said they, "Cheep-poo-astotin, you can't keep on crying for this little girl of yours that is dead. Why don't you try to get one of those young, pretty girls in the camp? Surely you can win one of them?"

But as not one of them had consented to give him a drink since the death of his little girl, he thought that it was hopeless. At once another scheme came to his mind. So he said to these two young men, "If you will go on a long trip with me, and help me to steal horses from other tribes of Indians, I will stop mourning."

These young boys consented because they had respect for Pointed Cap as a warrior. So away they went without the knowledge of anybody in the camp.

They travelled for a great many days. At last they came in sight of an Indian camp. "I will go to this camp," Pointed Cap told the lads, "stab as many of the people as I can, and drive their horses here where you will meet me."

And so he did. He stabbed fourteen of the bravest men in the camp, and drove their horses to his own camp. Among these horses were three fast runners. One of these he kept; the others he gave, one each, to his boys. Then he took the rest of the horses back to the camp of his people where he distributed them amongst the men. This was the law of the camp. Pointed Cap continued to steal until he got his camp well stocked with fine horses. He was a great horse thief, and at last he got a wife.

To return to our hunt. It was a quiet winter. The great buffalo herds, chased by the hunters, had gone south into American territory. It was too far for the half-breed hunters to follow, and, besides, they were not allowed to cross the line. Only the Indians were allowed to hunt on United States territory. Toward spring the herds came back to their grazing grounds. But the buffalo were really practically gone from the Canadian plains.

In the spring we went back to Fort Garry. I sold my robes and furs for two thousand five hundred dollars. My profit was only five hundred dollars. I didn't cover expenses. Still, I was travelling, and it was a good life.

CHAPTER NINE

Dumont's Brigade

The next year, in July, we started from Fort Garry and made for Batoche. The only crossing on the south branch of the Saskatchewan River was at this point, Batoche, so we made for it. It was the narrowest point in the river.

When we got there we made a ferryboat of our own. We took two big buffalo hides and soaked them properly. Then we stretched them on the ground and sewed them together with sinew. Next two large logs were hewn down on two sides to make them lighter. Over these logs, which were held apart by cross-pieces, we stretched the buffalo hides and lashed them tightly. The size of this raft, when finished, was twelve feet long, and ten feet wide. When the skins were dry, we rubbed buffalo tallow into the seams to make them water-tight. The tallow acted like pitch. We melted the tallow by holding it in our mouths. We let the raft dry for a day, after filling the seams, before using it.

Now, we attached heavy Hudson's Bay cord-line ropes to our barque, and one man swam the river with them. We ran our carts, one at a time, onto this ferryboat, and the men on the opposite bank pulled the raft across. We pulled it back. We must have had two hundred carts, and it took us three days to cross them. When we got all the carts across, we unfastened the hides and kept them for future use.

When we got across the river we went on to the Hudson's Bay Post at Fort Carlton. We wanted to buy some provisions as ours were getting low. But the buffalo were getting scarce, and we could get no pemmican at this post. However, the Factor[1] very kindly gave each family a little allowance. He showed no partiality. We stopped there for two days. At the end of that time we started for the plains to look for buffalo. For a time we were without success.

We travelled southward for two days, along the north branch of the Saskatchewan River towards Battleford. We met a small herd of buffalo. Those who had buffalo runners got on their backs and raced after the buffalo. An old Indian rode up to me after I had shot one buffalo. I asked the old Cree what he wanted. He told me he was camping near there and had nothing to eat. I told him to jump off his horse, help me skin the buffalo and I would give him half. The old fellow was proud and glad. His name was Cha-chetch (Stutter). We stopped there that day.

The next day we got to Battleford, Noo-tinto-see-pees the Indians called it. Then we went farther west and reached Sounding Lake. The next morning a man galloped up to our camp. We were getting buffalo now. I had been in two races and my share was twelve. We were skinning buffalo, and drying and curing the meat when this rider, who was Gabriel Dumont, came.

Dumont asked to see the Chief of our brigade, who was Charles Trottier. He had come to ask if he could join our camp. Trottier asked him how many families there were in his brigade. He replied that there were two half-breed families, and about twenty-five families of Indians. We had heard that Dumont's brigade had the smallpox. Trottier told him this and asked him why he didn't tell the truth like a man. Dumont replied that Trottier had not given him time to explain that only the two half-breed families did not have smallpox.[2]

1. Lawrence Clark was the Chief Factor at Fort Carlton. He was brother-in-law of the late Justice MacKay of the Saskatchewan Court of Appeal.
2. Father Constantine Scollen, missionary, in writing to Lieut.-Governor Laird of Manitoba from Fort Pitt on September 8, 1876, stated: "In 1870 came that disease so fatal to Indians, the smallpox, which told upon the Blackfeet with terrible effect, destroying between six hundred and eight hundred of

Trottier agreed to let Dumont and his two half-breed families join us in two or three days, if they hadn't developed the disease in that time. But he said that they could not come inside our camp. They must camp at a distance. In the meantime Trottier called a meeting and selected some head-men to keep a guard over Dumont's tents so that the occupants did not come too near.

Then the whole brigade arrived and wanted to come into our camp. Our Chief told us to take our guns and prevent them from doing this. We were ordered to shoot the first man that came near our camp. We kept Dumont's brigade half a mile away from us. But the beggars would come at night and wash their running sores in our spring water. Dumont was no kind of a leader, and I don't know how he got his reputation as one. He could not control his Indians.

Our Chief called a meeting, and we decided that we would dig four wells, one at each corner of the camp. The soil was sandy and it was easy to get water. We dug the wells, and at night four men were appointed to guard each well.

At the end of the third day, just before the two half-breed families were to be admitted to our camp, one of Gabriel's relations, a sister's child, died of smallpox. Because of that we could not let them in at all.

The Indians in Dumont's brigade had lots of furs and buffalo meat, but we didn't dare to trade with them. We gave them a few things that they needed—tea, sugar, and tobacco— but we could not afford to give them goods for nothing.

There was nobody to do anything for these Indians. There was no doctor, and they had black smallpox. Some days there were ten or twelve deaths. One day I visited their camp, and it was a pitiful sight. I was on horseback. Of course it was warm, being summer-time, but they lay all uncovered. Horrible cramps drew their bodies up until they rested on the tips of their heels and the tops of their heads. They died in agony. In one way these Indians were not to be pitied because they

them." The numbers of the Blackfeet had formerly been approximately 10,000 on the British side of the line.

had brought this disease upon themselves. We found out that they had come upon a camp of Blackfoot Indians who were suffering with this disease, had raided it, and had carried away their women and children.

By this time we were quite well loaded up with pemmican and dried meat that we had got ourselves. There were about twenty-five or twenty-eight families in our brigade, so Charles Trottier said that we had better go back to Round Plain in order to get rid of Dumont's brigade. We did. Soon after we reached our wintering place, a message came from Dumont, who was at Batoche, asking Trottier to send some rum or alcohol. Alcohol was the only treatment they knew of for smallpox. They wanted ten gallons.

It appears that after we separated from him, Dumont had got into the camp of his father at Batoche where they had smallpox. Trottier came to me and said that, since his house was not finished, he could not spare his time or that of his men to take the alcohol. My house was completed. He wondered if I would make the trip to Batoche, a distance of sixty miles. It would take four days to go there and back. I agreed to go if my wife had no objection.

I started with the alcohol. They were very glad to see me! Some were better. Before I entered the camp, I took a big glass of liquor. That was what the doctors advised long ago. They said it would keep one from getting the disease. I saw a woman, Dumont's sister-in-law, who was recovering from the disease. She was covered with scabs. They would not come off, so her husband took his pocket knife and cut off the scabs that completely covered the soles of her feet. It was getting cold now and the disease was dying out.

The buffalo were disappearing fast, and there was not much trading, not enough to pay for our outfit. In the spring of 1872 I decided not to go back to Fort Garry but to go to Fort Qu'Appelle. So I came to Lebret, called after Pierre Lebret, a priest, where I now live.

When we got here, we found the people all starving. There was a scattered settlement here, as there was around all the old Hudson's Bay posts, of about four or five hundred people. They were half-breed hunters mostly. These settlers had nothing to eat but dried fish.

We had word from Isaac Cowie—clerk in charge of the Hudson's Bay Company post at Fort Qu'Appelle, while the Chief Factor, Archibald MacDonald, was at Fort Ellice—that no furs brought in from the West were to be taken to Fort Garry. They were afraid smallpox would be carried in the furs.

Well, I had some fine robes. I think I had about seventy buffalo robes, and about two hundred dollars worth of small furs. Charles Trottier, refusing to believe that the brigades had been forbidden to go to Fort Garry, decided to leave his family at Lebret and go on. I asked him if he would buy my furs and take them with him. They were good furs, and I did not want them on my hands. I agreed to let him have the buffalo robes for five dollars apiece, and the other furs for a hundred and fifty dollars. He was willing to do this, but said that he would not be able to pay me until he came back. I knew he was good for it so I was satisfied.

I stayed at Lebret for two weeks, and then started for the plains again to hunt buffalo and buy up dried meat and pemmican. It was a good trip. I came back to Fort Qu'Appelle with ten carts loaded with as much meat as the horses could draw. I had travelled over the plains in the direction of Cypress Hills, and Wood Mountain. I sold all that meat to Cowie for twelve hundred dollars. At that time meat did not fetch a very good price.

I came back to my camp at Lebret, down where the graveyard is now, on the south-east quarter of Lebret cemetery, and asked my wife if she would be willing to go on ahead to our wintering place at Round Plain while I went to Fort Garry for supplies. It was now the beginning of August. My wife started for Round Plain, and I for Fort Garry.

When I reached Fort Garry, I settled up the few accounts I had, and then bought a thousand dollars worth of goods. I paid cash for it, and started for Round Plain.

I reached my wintering place. My wife, according to my

orders, had taken her men and had gone across the river to hunt. All the brigade was gone. My old mother-in-law was keeping house and watching the stuff. That night it was very cold. It was now the beginning of November, and the river froze over. I decided to cross the river on foot to see if the hunters were still on the west side of the river. I took a pole with me so that if the ice broke I could throw it across to bear me up. I got across safely, and went to where I thought the hunters would be. All were gone but my camp. They had lost a horse that morning and had stayed behind to find it. Just as I arrived, one of my men galloped up with the horse.

I directed my men to hitch up and go on. The next day I hitched up my horse and cart, and overtook the hunters at a place called Little Devil's Lake. The following day we moved farther on, and ran into a band of buffalo. We stopped at that camp for ten days. We ran buffalo every day. We had struck a great band of buffalo, and we were right in their path for they were travelling west.

It was getting late and cold now, so we decided to go back to Round Plains. We passed the winter there. In January or February of that year I attended a Giving Away Dance. I have given a description of it earlier in the book.

In the spring of the year we were allowed to go back to Fort Garry to sell furs. I did not get a very big price for mine. Buyers were still afraid of smallpox. I made about two thousand dollars out of my entire outfit.

Chapter Ten

The Legend of Naheyow

O ften for pastime, in the winter when things were quiet, two or three of us would go to visit an old Indian called The Rump (Tapapachakonap). He belonged to One Arrow's band. It was a big camp of fifty lodges not very far from our wintering place.

Now the older an Indian grows the more respected he becomes in the tribe. His stories are worth listening to. The Rump was a great story-teller. Always I took him a present of tea, tobacco, sugar, and sometimes a bannock. Then I would say to him, "Here, my grandfather, what do you know? You are old, you must know something."

One day he told me the story of the Pointed Cap. He said, "Once there was an Indian named Chee-poo-astotin (the Pointed Cap).[1] He was a great warrior, a great brave, in his day. He was shot by the Blackfoot Indians. When Pointed Cap went on the war-path, he left behind him a wife and a little boy named Naheyow. The little boy grew up. One day he asked his mother where his father was. She told him that he had gone on a war party and had been shot by the Blackfoot tribe.

"When Naheyow became a brave he said to his mother, 'Na-ka, I want you to fix up a lot of moccasins for me.'

"When his mother asked him what he wanted the moccasins for, he replied that he was going to war with the Blackfoot Indians. His mother coaxed him not to go, but Naheyow answered that he would never be satisfied until he had taken

1. Father of the Pointed Cap I knew.

some Blackfoot scalps. His grandfather said, 'Let him go O-tah-ne-sha (my daughter).'

"The old man asked Naheyow how many braves he was taking in his war party. The boy answered that he was going alone. Then he asked his mother to pack his moccasins. He would leave that night, he said, because none of the tribe must know where he was going. He went.

"That night a big storm came, a blizzard. It was towards spring and the snow fell heavily. He travelled on through the snow. No one could track him in the drifts. In the morning all the young warriors turned out to look for him, but his tracks had disappeared.

"Naheyow got to the southern branch of the Saskatchewan, to the forks of the Red Deer. He was in the Blackfoot country. Now, he thought to himself, it is time for me to prepare for a fight. He shot a buffalo, skinned it, and took the best part of the carcass to his little camp. He had no tent. He roasted quite a bit of meat, and packed enough to last him for two or three days. He took as much as he could carry on his back with his gun and ammunition.

"Then he set out to look for his enemies. He travelled up the Red Deer River, and from the high bank he saw ahead of him a big Blackfoot camp. There were tall, large pine trees sloping down the banks to the river, so Naheyow decided to hide under one of the trees, and to stay concealed as long as his grub lasted. It was a good place from which to spy on his enemies to find out when to attack them.

"By and by he saw two persons on horseback—one was leading a horse—coming to where he was lying under the tree. They came to the foot of the bank and dismounted. A tent was strapped to the back of the third horse, and on top of this tent a woman sat. They pitched their tent. The Indian went off and shot a buffalo from a band that was feeding nearby.

"After watching this party for a day or two, Naheyow encountered the young Blackfoot. He discovered that he was the son of the Chief. When the young Blackfoot asked him who he was, Naheyow said that he was the son of Pointed Cap who had been killed by the Blackfoot tribe, and that he had come to avenge his father's death. The Chief's son said, 'I'm glad to meet you. You must be a brave man and a good-natured man. I won't kill you, but you may kill me.'

"Naheyow replied that it would be no satisfaction to kill one man and two women. He wanted, he said, to tackle the whole camp. The young Blackfoot asked Naheyow to stay with his wife, and sister, while he went back to the camp to tell his father that Pointed Cap's son was here. When Naheyow agreed, the young brave threw the saddle on his horse and away he went.

"When the rider reached his father's camp, he told the Chief that Naheyow had come to avenge the death of his father, Pointed Cap. He explained that Naheyow had had a chance to kill him while he was on his honeymoon trip, but had not done so because he wanted to attack the band. The Chief replied that this young Cree must be a very brave man. That was what counted with the Indians—bravery.

"The young Blackfoot asked his father to let Naheyow come into the camp, and to promise faithfully not to let any of the tribe kill him. The old Chief promised. Then he commanded one of his chief headmen to get on horseback and to ride around the whole camp—there were over one hundred lodges—to notify all the braves that a young Cree was coming into the camp, and to forbid anyone to touch him.

"A council of headmen was held. All agreed not to kill the Cree. Then, the Chief ordered twenty of his braves to mount their horses and go with his son to meet Naheyow. Also he ordered them to saddle and take one of the best horses for their guest.

"The Blackfoot riders greeted Naheyow, put him on horseback and galloped back—about ten or fifteen miles—to their camp. The young Blackfoot rode beside Naheyow, and, when they dismounted, he took him by the hand, led him to his father's tent, and placed him on a fine rush-covered seat which had been specially prepared for him.

"There was a big stir in the camp. The braves were very

much excited. They hated the Crees. The first headman wanted to kill Naheyow. The young Cree said to the Chief, 'Let the headman come and kill me. If he is brave enough, let him step up.'

"The headman stepped up. He held a long butcher knife in his hand. Naheyow pulled his shirt open, bared his breast and said, 'Stab me right here in the heart.'

"The headman stepped up, and then fell on his knees. 'Ha-ha-ha! Is that the kind of braves you have here?' asked Naheyow. But they didn't kill him. Before Naheyow's arrival the Chief had selected one of the very best tents they had in the camp and had it pitched beside his own for the new-comer.

"When night came the Chief said to his guest, 'You'll be my son-in-law. I'll give you my daughter.'

"Now, the Chief got up and addressed his Indians. He said, 'I've met lots and lots of brave men but never one as brave as Naheyow. I'm going to have him for my son-in-law. I dare any of my band to injure or offend him. If any of you dare to hurt him you will have me to deal with.'

"Naheyow and the Chief's daughter were married in Indian fashion. They lived in the Blackfoot encampment. After a while a son was born to them. Then two strange Indians came to the Chief's camp. It seems that the Chief was threatened by another band of Indians. These messengers carried tobacco (wa-pa-kin-a-kin) and gave it to the Chief. This meant a challenge of war. It was from a very strong nation called the Mandan. They were strong in numbers and very cruel. The place for the fight was set.

"Naheyow noticed that his wife and all the Indians looked downhearted when they saw these messengers. He asked why they looked nervous. His wife told him that her father had been notified that the Mandans were taking the war-path against him. They were strong, and he was afraid he would get beaten.

"'Ho-ha-ha! If that is all that troubles your father, I'll soon fix that. Go and tell your father that if he will give me twenty of his best horses and men—I don't want all the men in the camp—I'll go and fix the Mandan Chief,' laughed Naheyow.

"This message pleased the Chief. He said, 'Tell your husband to come here. We will talk.'

"He told Naheyow to choose his own braves. He said that twenty warriors were not enough. The young Cree answered that he did not want to be bothered with men. Twenty would be enough.

"The next morning Naheyow chose his warriors and started out to meet the big party of Mandan braves. They went to the valley that had been selected for a fighting ground.

"When they were descending to the valley, Naheyow said to his men, 'Let me make a rush at them alone.' And so they did.

"Before half the day was over, they had killed all the Mandans that were worth killing. There must have been two or three hundred Mandans against twenty Blackfeet. They fought with bows and arrows, knives, axes, and tomahawks, whatever they could lay their hands on. Naheyow returned to his camp. Not one of his men was wounded.

"The old Chief began to think that he had a very brave man for a son-in-law. He decided to give him the Chiefship. All the braves in the camp were afraid of Naheyow, but they respected him like a king. He became Chief.

"One day when he was sitting in his tent, he looked so sad that his wife asked him what the matter was. He told her that it had been a long time since he had seen his mother. His grandfather, he thought, must be dead, but he would like to see his mother before she died.

"Naheyow's wife went to her father's tent and told him how sad her husband was, and that he wanted to go and see his mother who was old and alone. The old Chief said, 'Good. That is what I wanted long ago. Now this will give us a chance to make a treaty with the Crees. Naheyow is the Chief. He can go and take all the men he likes with him. As well, he can take fifty horses—loose horses, not those they are riding.'

"Naheyow started with twenty-five mounted braves, and a band of fifty loose horses. These horses were for a gift to the Cree band to which his mother belonged.

"When Naheyow found the camp where he thought his mother might be, he asked his wife and the warriors to remain where they were. He went ahead to find out if his mother were still living. When he reached the camp, nobody knew him. He entered the tent, and asked if Pointed Cap's wife was still living. The old wives and the old men began to wonder who this brave was that was dressed like a Blackfoot. They told him that Pointed Cap's widow was still alive, but that she was very old. He asked about his grandfather.

"'You are Naheyow,' they cried, jumping up to kiss him, and to welcome him back.

"Naheyow told them that he had a party of twenty-five men, his wife, and a band of fifty loose horses about fifteen miles away. He asked if he could bring them to the camp. He greeted his old mother. The Chief of this band of Crees selected ten men to accompany him and escort his people to the Cree camp. It was quite an imposing procession—the Cree and the Blackfoot tribes marching together.

"The next day the fifty horses were distributed among the band on condition that there would be no more fighting between the two tribes. The treaty of peace was made. That ended the wars between the two bands."

That treaty must have been made about one hundred years ago. It is nearly seventy years since The Rump told me that story.

CHAPTER ELEVEN

The Building of Fort Walsh

The next year I took out an outfit worth eighteen hundred dollars from Fort Garry. I had been long enough on the Round Plain. I thought I would make a change, take a trip south to the Cypress Hills, now Fort Walsh. I put up a house for the winter in what was called the Four-Mile Coulee. The Indians called it Wa-pa-tou-nis-ou-see-peesis.

It was a fine open fall. About the beginning of December we made a good hunt. Alone, I shot over one hundred buffalo. We had good weather to dry and cure our meat.

One day we were busy baling and packing our meat when three red coats rode up. One of them stepped up and spoke to me in English, asked me if there was anyone in the brigade who could speak English. I told him that he had the right man. Then I asked him what he wanted to know. He told me that he wanted two interpreters, one that could speak English and French, and one that could speak English and Blackfoot. I told him that I could get them for him. Then I told him that my name was Norbert Welsh.

"I'm Major Walsh so we might be related," he replied.

I told him that I did not think we were, and asked him what he was going to do. He answered that he was going out to the Blackfoot camp[1] and wanted to know how far it was. The country was not surveyed at this time, but I told him that

---

1. There would be between four and five hundred Blackfoot Indians in this encampment.

it must be about one hundred and fifty miles from where we were. Then he asked me if I would pick two interpreters to accompany him. I said that I would and asked him if he would come with me to the tents of the men.

He jumped off his horse, threw his reins to one of his men, and together we walked to the tent of Batoche La Bombarbe. I asked La Bombarbe if he would hire, as an interpreter of Blackfoot and English, to Major Walsh on a trip to the Blackfoot camp. He agreed. Then we went to the tent of Joseph Levielle and asked him if he would go as an interpreter in English and French. He said he would. The next day Major Walsh called for these men. He had a good sized troop, about fifty or sixty mounted policemen.

When he was leaving Major Walsh said, "Welsh, I will see you again when I come back from the Blackfoot camp. I want to establish a fort here at the Cypress Hills."

We had now finished our hunt, so we went back to the Cypress Hills. We were about two days' travel away, about forty or fifty miles. I selected a place in a big coulee, which we called the Four-Mill-Coulee, for our wintering place. There were about sixty families in this brigade.

By and by we heard that Major Walsh was back from the Blackfoot country. He came and selected a place about four miles from where we were. We were on the north side of the hills. He went to the south side and built a fort, and put up a log building for himself and his men. He stayed at this fort most of the time.

Soon a big American company came and started a store at Cypress Hills. A man named Baker Clarke,[2] was at the head of the company. Another big company, T.C. Power & Company, also started a store. And all the traders trying to do business around this post. I tell you it was very hard now to get a robe from the Indians or half-breeds. Prices went up. The stores had a greater variety of goods to offer than the traders. But just the same I managed to get my share.

2. Probably J.G. Baker & Co., and Messrs. T.C. Power & Bro. They had stores at Fort Walsh in 1876, at the time the Blackfoot Treaty was made.

The last of March, we left our houses and made for Fort Garry, planning to call at Lebret on our way. I had a hundred and twenty good robes, three thousand pounds of pemmican, and a thousand pounds of dried meat. When we got to Fort Ellice I met the Chief Factor, Archibald MacDonald. I knew him very well. He asked me if I had good robes. He had passed us on the road the day before, and had admired a fine grey horse that my wife was driving in her democrat. MacDonald said, when he had come to my camp that night, that he had a horse like my grey horse that he would like to match. He asked me if I would sell mine. I told him that I would. Then he asked me how much I wanted. I said that he could make me an offer.

"How would a hundred and seventy-five dollars suit you?" he asked.

"The horse is yours," I said.

"Welsh, about your robes. I am sure they are good, for when you say a thing is good it is always good. You had better sell them to me," he continued.

I told him that I would be very foolish to sell them now when you might say I was in Fort Garry, only one hundred and fifteen miles from it.

"I'm going to tell you, my dear friend, that I have just returned from Fort Garry. The robes are fetching no price there. Another thing, after you pass Birtle, you'll get into mud and pools of water all the way to Portage-la-Prairie. I have just bought a horse from you. Why not sell me your whole outfit?" MacDonald wanted to know.

I asked him what he would give me. Since the robes were worth nothing in Fort Garry, I thought that they would be worth far less here.

"Welsh, take down a package of your furs, not the best. I know you have them separated, so show me one bale of next to the best," he replied.

I ordered my man to bring down a bale of robes from a certain cart. I put my knife into the package and cut the string. There were ten robes in each package. He examined them.

I asked him how he liked them. He said if they all averaged like that he would give me twelve dollars apiece for them. Again I asked him how he could afford to pay me twelve dollars apiece for robes that were worth nothing in Fort Garry.

"My dear friend," he said, "I'm the Hudson's Bay Company. You need not sell your robes to me unless you like, but I am offering you all they are worth this year. They may be worth more next year but you can't hold them over. But the Hudson's Bay Company can hold them as long as they like. Deliver them to the Hudson's Bay Company at Fort Garry or leave them here, and I will pay you twelve dollars a robe. I'll bet you won't get more from them from any other buyer."

I asked him what about my pemmican and dried meat. He said he would take that too, as they needed some then, and would pay me in goods, at wholesale prices. He offered me fifteen cents a pound for pemmican and dried meat. For the furs he would pay cash. Well, that was fairly good. I decided to sell. Four thousand pounds of pemmican at fifteen cents a pound made six hundred dollars, and I got fourteen hundred dollars for the robes. MacDonald wanted me to go back to the plains to get more pemmican for him, but I had business at Fort Garry so had to go on there.

I can assure you that MacDonald was right about the road. The fellows with loads had a job. I frequently said to my wife as I saw them struggling through the mud that even if I had sold my goods to MacDonald five hundred dollars cheaper than the Fort Garry price, it still would have paid me.

We got to Fort Garry. The other traders began to sell their furs. The highest price they got for their robes was ten dollars apiece. MacDonald was a good friend to me. He often said to me that he would always do what was right with me, and that I would always find him honest. I bought what stuff I wanted and returned to Fort Ellice. This was about May. I took my dried meat money in trade.

There were so many traders out on the plains that I took out on this trip only fifteen hundred dollars worth of goods. I reached Fort Qu'Appelle about the 15th of July, 1875, and went on to my place at Lebret which was about five miles from the fort. I stopped at Lebret for the rest of July.

At the beginning of August I thought I would take a trip around the plains, buy some dried meat and sell to MacDonald again. He was the Chief Factor over all these Hudson's Bay Posts, Fort Pelly, Fort Ellice, Riding Mountain, Touchwood Hills, and Swan River. I went. I was away twenty days. I brought in five thousand pounds of pemmican and dried meat, and sold it to Isaac Cowie at Fort Qu'Appelle for fifteen cents a pound. I took half cash, and half trade at wholesale price, remember, freight paid.

After the first of October, we started off to Cypress Hills to our winter house. We had left a good winter house there, and also about a dozen horses on the plains. When we got to Cypress, I mudded up my house and my store-house. I had everything fixed up by the beginning of November.

CHAPTER TWELVE

Welsh's "Crazy Race"

little later I got ready to go on a hunting party. I persuaded four other families to join us. That made five families in my brigade. I wanted to handle this in my own way, to be the Boss, and I didn't want a big crowd. We started. After two days' travel, we came to a tract of land where the buffalo were pasturing. They were travelling westward. I told my friends that we had better stop here. There was water and lots of feed. It was well sheltered, and would be a good camping spot.

The next morning, I saw, about three miles from our camp, a big herd of buffalo. I was an early riser. The occupants of the other tents were still asleep. I wakened them, and told them to hurry through breakfast as we would have a good buffalo race that morning.

After breakfast we saddled our horses, and away we went to where the buffalo were grazing. We chased them, but somehow we did not make a very good run. All we got, the five of us, was fifty buffalo. That was not worthwhile.

When we returned to camp, the women laughed, because we had killed so few buffalo. They told us that they had nothing to do, that fixing five or six buffalo apiece was nothing.

Then next day the same thing happened. When I got up, I saw a big herd of buffalo travelling straight toward us. We were camped right on a buffalo pass. We told the women that we were not going to kill many buffalo that day, because it would be too much work for them to fix the hides. We got sixty.

For three days after that we saw no buffalo. This gave us time to take care of the hides of the buffalo we had already killed. There was still no buffalo on the fourth day. My comrades said that the herd must have travelled on, that we would see no more buffalo for a while. I told them that we would not move yet, that we would wait another day.

The next morning, as usual, I was the first up. About a mile from our camp, I saw a big band of buffalo lying down. The wind was contrary. They didn't scent us. They were at the very top of the hill.

I wakened my men. After breakfast we mounted our horses and started. I ordered my men to ride to the other side of the hill and come on to them from the opposite direction. We did. Before the buffalo could get up, we were in amongst them with our horses. They were surprised and terrified, and instead of taking the direction in which we tried to drive them, out on the level prairie on top of the hill, they all galloped down the hill, which was very steep.

I had a very fast buffalo runner, but he was strong-headed. I tried to stop him but couldn't. The other riders reined in their horses. When I couldn't hold mine—he was right in among the buffalo, galloping with them—I thought, well I'm as good as dead anyway. I'll take the chance! So I gave him a tip with my halter-shank to make him jump down the hill as far as possible. Still on my horse, I landed part way down the hill and went galloping on with the herd.

I pulled out my repeating rifle and began shooting into the herd. When I was through shooting, I tied my horse to the head of the last buffalo I had shot. I looked around and saw a great many dead buffalo. My friends, I thought, must surely have come down with me and shot some of them. As I looked for the other hunters, I counted the dead and dying buffalo. There were twenty.

In a few minutes my wife's uncle, Joe Boyer, came galloping down. He was surprised that I was still alive, and told me that only "a dang fool of a man" would do what I had done, whip up his horse and gallop downhill with a herd of furious buffalo. I asked him how many buffalo he and the others had shot. When he answered that they had shot none, I asked him who had shot all the buffalo. He said that I had shot them all.

Then I said: "I will show you what a fool will do. There are twenty buffalo here. You take four, and the other three men will take four each. I will take four."

He replied, "Welsh, we can't get ahead of you."

The other three men rode up. The dying buffalo were rolling around my horse's legs. But a trained buffalo horse could generally keep out of the way of furious or wounded buffalo. We finished killing, and skinned the buffalo.

Then I looked at my rifle. I still had three cartridges left, in the chamber which held fourteen. I had killed twenty buffalo. In my excitement, I must have re-loaded my gun unconsciously. I examined my cartridge belt. It was short ten cartridges. I had no recollection of having re-loaded my gun. My comrades of long ago called this, "Welsh's Crazy Race."

The best buffalo runner I ever owned was a horse I bought from a horse trader named Belanger. He was a Bay with a white strip down his forehead. I called him "Brake." I never knew how fast he could run until one day when the curiosity of the other hunters got the best of them. Some of the hunters were a little jealous, and they wanted to know who really had the fastest horse in the brigade. My brother-in-law, François Boyer, came and told me that a group of hunters, who thought they had better horses than mine, were proposing secretly to get together, and, asking me to join them, scare the buffalo from a long distance, speed their horses and reach the buffalo before me. I thought to myself, I'll fix their little plot. There were about forty hunters in this scheme—all with fast runners. The men were Thomas and John Beaulieu, Charles, André, and Antoine Trottier, James Swain, and many others.

When we were all together at the appointed time a shot was fired from a mile away. The buffalo started to run. We shot after them. I reached the herd first, shot a buffalo in the hind legs, cut him out of the herd, chased him back to meet the other hunters, called to one of my men to finish the animal, turned, and was again amongst the herd and had shot four more buffalo before my friends got there. The only time I ever laid a lash to that buffalo runner was on that day. After I left the wounded buffalo with my man, I gave my horse a tip. He leaped over the prairie like a crazy thing. I paid forty buffalo robes for that horse. I broke and trained him for buffalo-running myself. Of all the horses that I owned and rode, I never had a runner that could race like this one. After the buffalo were gone, I sold him to a man named McPherson for two hundred and fifty dollars. The horse changed hands several times until the late Dr. M.M. Seymour got him. He used him for a saddle-horse to go around and visit his patients. This was in the eighties when he was stationed at Lebret.

We stayed in this camp for a month. We were shooting buffalo every day, from twenty to forty of them. When we came to pack up, I had for my share, cut up and packed, one hundred and twenty buffalo. The other fellows didn't have that many. They had from twenty to fifty apiece. Each man's share was what he had killed himself, except in the crazy race when I had shared my kill with my companions.

I loaded my carts as high as I could pack them. I had ten carts loaded with robes, meat, and fat. I had two hundred pounds of marrow fat. We boiled the buffalo fat on the plains, poured it into a buffalo hide, and let it freeze. We got back to Four-Mile Coulee, and I put all my stuff under lock and key. I had a hired man, always, so we hauled plenty of dry wood to the door. Now I thought, I'll just make one more hunting trip this winter.

We made two other hunts that fall when we needed fresh meat. I started out again on the first one with my brother-in-law, Frank Boyer. On the second day of our travel, we came upon a band of buffalo. They were travelling. My heavens, but it was blowing! It was late November, but there was no snow. It was blowing so hard that we could scarcely get on horseback. We were travelling west towards Calgary. I told Boyer that he had better take the horse, and I would take the mare. The mare could run faster, but the horse was longer winded, and Frank was the better shot. We went after the buffalo. I shot one, and my mare got out of wind and dropped behind. Boyer went on over a little hill with the buffalo. When I overtook him, he had dismounted and was standing beside his horse. He had shot eleven buffalo. We decided that the twelve buffalo would be enough for this trip. We had a man with us so we started to skin the buffalo and get everything ready for the next morning.

When we got back to our little camp, we found that our tent had blown down. We set it up again, and spread our meat out to cool. The next morning was cold. The meat was stiff but not well frozen. We decided to make for home. We packed the meat, and buffalo hides in our carts. It took us two days to get home. We had had to travel quite far to find the buffalo. Everybody in the wintering place was out of fresh meat. I told my wife that if anybody wanted fresh meat she should give it to them. But when night came all my fresh meat was gone! Well, I had offered them meat, and I couldn't say anything.

In December, there was snow but I told my brother-in-law that I thought we should go off on another little hunt. When other men saw us going, they made up their minds to follow. By the time we reached the plains there were quite a lot of us, about twenty or twenty-five hunters.

We travelled for two days. On the second day, after dinner, we came on a band of buffalo. There were thousands of them. In the first race, I killed all that I needed to fill my five carts. I told my brother-in-law that I had enough—green meat from fifteen buffalo—and would go home. He could do as he wished.

I went out again about the beginning of February, 1876. I shot six buffalo and brought all the meat home. We were provided with fresh frozen meat for the remainder of the winter. I told my man that all I would have to do for the remainder of the winter would be to look after the horses;

they were pasturing on the open plains. His duties were to go every day and round them up, cut wood, and make fires.

I was very fine at this time, making a big splash. Before leaving Fort Garry on this trip, I had bought a stove from James H. Ashdown, the hardware man, with all the equipment for it—a tea-kettle, frying pans, a steamer for potatoes, and all the other things that went with it. When the Indians saw it, they thought it very wonderful. They asked me what I called it in Cree. I told them "Coota-wana-pisk," which meant cooking stove. This stove made my house the most important one in the brigade on the wintering ground. All the women came to our house to bake bread. The Indians came to trade, and to see the stove.

CHAPTER THIRTEEN

Building a Log Chapel

The winter of 1876 we got word that a priest, a travelling missionary, was coming from sixty miles away, from the east end of the Cypress Hills, to visit us. I asked my uncle, Charles Trottier, if it would not be wise, since we had such a large population of children, and no religious instruction, to call a meeting and try to arrange to build a church. He agreed, so we called a meeting. It was decided to build a chapel.

The next morning each man took his axe and began to chop trees. There were about twelve men chopping trees, and twelve more hauling the logs to where we intended to build the chapel, the first in this part of the country. In two days we had everything ready to start building.

We built the chapel sixty feet long by thirty feet broad, with a wall twelve feet high, and a peaked roof. The roof sticks were pine logs split in two, and hewn. We hewed pine logs for a floor, and we made a fine floor. When the chapel was finished, we said that every man would have to build his own pew. In a week we had the whole interior finished except for the plastering. When there are a lot of men with a good will, they can do a big job in a day. Charles Trottier said that the plastering could be done in two days, and asked who would go for the priest.

Sixty miles across country in deep snow—there was no road—was quite a trip, but I told the traders that if they would let me have a man to accompany me, I would supply everything else, and would go to fetch the priest. My sister-in-law was married to a man named John Tanner. He offered to go.

The next morning we started. We travelled fifty miles that day before camping for the night. We finished our trip in the morning. We rested at the end of the Cypress Hills that day, and next morning we started back with the priest. It took us four days to make the round trip. The church that we built that winter stood until 1928, when it was burned down.

My house there at Cypress Hills is still up. In all I must have had about twenty wintering houses on the Saskatchewan plains.

The priest, whose name was Father Genie stopped with us for two months. He baptised a great many children. He baptised my oldest son. We had a lot of weddings too. We had a grand time dancing, eating, and visiting. For those that wanted liquor, there was plenty. But the traders never drank much, just enough to be sociable.

That spring we came back to Lebret. Fort Qu'Appelle was growing to be a big post now. I brought back a lot of pemmican and dried meat, and sold it to the Hudson's Bay Company for eleven hundred dollars. I did not have more than fifty robes. At Cypress, I had traded four hundred dollars worth of furs for ten horses. I brought back with me from the Cypress hills seven dead bodies for burial at Lebret.

One was that of a man who had gone out on the prairie to look for his horses, had got lost, and had frozen to death. One was the body of Charles Trottier's fourteen year old boy. The other five bodies were those of children from one to five years of age. The bodies were frozen. I made the coffins myself, and placed the bodies in them. It was painful to think of one's children and friends being buried out on the prairie. In all my trading trips, from Round Plain and all over, I brought in over sixty bodies and buried them in the cemetery at Lebret.

When I got the bodies from Cypress Hills to Lebret, I paid a man to dig one big grave. Then I laid the bodies into it side by side. In the morning I got a priest to hold a service over them. I paid him five dollars.

We stayed at Lebret for a while, then I started back to Cypress Hills to buy meat, but on my way, and before I got there, I had loaded up with pemmican and some robes. I suppose the buffalo were already getting scarce. When I got to an Indian camp and found forty or fifty men making pemmican, each one sold me only a bag; that would make forty or fifty bags in a day.

I came back to Fort Qu'Appelle with a big load of pemmican, about six thousand pounds, and sold it to Cowie for fifteen cents a pound. I rested for a few days and planned what to do next. Then I told my wife that there was something I wanted in Fort Garry, and that she could stay at Lebret until I came back. I said that we would go back to the Cypress Hills as soon as I got back. She agreed. I sold my furs in Fort Garry and made another good deal. I got the same price for my robes, though they were not such good ones as the year before, fifteen dollars apiece, ten hundred and fifteen dollars in all. I made the round trip in thirty days. I had ten carts and a boy with me. The carts were loaded. I brought back fifty sacks of flour. These were one hundred pound sacks.

When I got back to Lebret, my wife, who had not been feeling very well, asked me to do her a favor. She said that since we had been married we had always worked together, but this winter she did not want to go back to Cypress. She wished to stay at Lebret.

I told her, very well, that we would stay at Lebret. And so we did. Now I had to find a place to rent or buy. I saddled my horse, jumped on his back, and rode to where the grain elevators stand to-day, perhaps a little further down. I asked a half-breed, Joseph Pelltier, who had a little house there with a store-house attached, if he would sell his house. It was worth about a hundred dollars. The traders were like one big family. They treated, and addressed each other as if they were related.

He said, "Oh, my nephew, I'm getting old. If I sell, I won't have time to build again before winter comes."

I asked, "How would two hundred dollars suit you?"

"Poverty is a hard master. You can have the house," he answered. I paid him the money, and moved into the house. We passed the winter there.

I traded here all winter. I had lots of goods, and I bought a lot from other traders. I decided to give up hunting as the buffalo had practically gone. I sold most of my horses. The Indians and half-breeds came to my place on the flats to trade.

About the tenth of September, 1877, I set out for Wood Mountain with a boy, a buffalo runner, and five carts. It was very cold when I started, blowing, and cold enough for snow. When I got to Willow Bunch it began to storm. About two feet of snow fell. There were about sixty or seventy wintering houses, traders' houses, here. I stayed in the wintering camp. Joseph La Bonbarbe told the others that they had me fixed, that I couldn't get away with my fine carts through the deep snow.

Batiste La Boucan (The Smoke) said that I had got the carts wholesale, and asked how much I would take for one. Sixty dollars, in pemmican and dried meat, I told him. Others traders wanted the carts cheaper. I wouldn't sell.

Then Indian summer came. Away went the snow. I packed my carts with pemmican, and dried meat, and made for Lebret. On my way back, I saw a little herd of seven buffalo. I got on my runner and after them. When I overtook them, only three were worth shooting. The others were too lean.

CHAPTER FOURTEEN

My Friend, Chief Starblanket

When the spring of 1878 came, I thought I would take a little run around on the plains to the Cypress Hills, to see if I could get some buffalo meat. I also wanted to do a little trading.

I packed up my outfit. I took ten carts and two men with me, or rather a man and a boy. When we got to Cypress we didn't see a buffalo, an Indian, or anything. Everything was bare. I told my man that there was no use travelling farther, and that he was to stay here with the boy and the outfit. In the morning I took my saddle-horse and went toward the Milk River to see if there was anybody there. It was quite a distance, but I knew that I could get there and back in one day.

I must have galloped about fifteen miles when I came to a small Indian camp. There were about twenty-five tents, that is about twenty-five families. This was Starblanket's camp. They gave the war-whoop and began to sing; they were pleased to see me because I had traded with them before. Starblanket said to his people: "It is the will of the Manitou that Wa-ka-kootchick turned up at our camp to-day. Now we can get something to live on."

They had nothing at all. No ammunition, no tea, no tobacco—nothing. I cross-questioned them about the buffalo, trying to find out where they had gone. There were no buffalo, they said, between there and across the Missouri River, whither all the hunters, Indians, half-breeds and traders, had chased them.

I asked them how long it would take me to reach the hunting camp across the Missouri. I thought I would go on horseback to find out what was going on. Starblanket said that, although I had a good horse that would take me to the river in a day, he would not advise me to go. He told me that I would have to swim the Missouri because the water had risen very high since the hunters had gone across. Also he said that he did not know how far beyond the river the hunters had travelled.

I could take Starblanket's word about the location of the hunters. I began to consider a little. If the Yankee traders caught an English trader on their territory (they didn't mind the Indians) they would seize him. I thought I had better not risk swimming the river, finding the hunters, or getting into trouble, and that I had better go back from here.

But first I wanted to see what Starblanket had. They were not hungry, as they had a little meat for themselves, but they had none to sell. I asked Starblanket if he had anything at all to sell. He said they had some skins for making moccasins, some sinews, and lots of shaggannappi (in those days we used shaggannappi instead of ropes).

I asked him to bring his stuff, and to let me see what it looked like. He had some fairly good leather. Everything was in such good shape that if I bought, I could sell it again.

Starblanket wanted to know where my camp was, and my outfit. I had brought my dinner with me. I told him that after dinner I would go back and get my outfit and bring it to his camp.

He clapped his hands, and said that I had always been a good man, and that I had not lost my goodness.

I hurried back to where my men were waiting. We hitched up, started for Starblanket's camp, and got there at twelve o'clock that night.

Early the next morning I took out a pound of tea, a couple of pounds of sugar, and a fathom of rope tobacco, and gave them to Starblanket. I told him to divide these things among his men, and to let them have a good drink of tea, and a good smoke, then we would trade.

I bought about a hundred and fifty dollars worth of stuff. By that time the Indians had quite a little supply of things, but not enough. They wanted more tea, tobacco, and ammunition.

Starblanket told me that I had lots of supplies, things they wanted, and that it was a pity to let me go away with all that stuff. I asked him what he meant, and if he meant to rob me. He replied that that was something he would never do, but that about the beginning of August they would all be going to Fort Qu'Appelle to get their treaty money.

Then I understood what was coming—he wanted credit from me. Starblanket was one of the first Chiefs. He had signed the Qu'Appelle treaty. It was June now, and the treaty money would be paid in August.

I asked him if it was credit that he wanted. He said it was. Then I told him that no trader could give an Indian credit on the expectation of collecting his bill when treaty money was paid. He agreed, but said that he and I were as one—that we were brothers. He always called me his brother. Then he asked me why he should take goods from me and not expect to pay.

"What you say is true, Starblanket," I answered. "You wouldn't want to take advantage of me. I have always been good to you, and to all the Indians. But if I were to give you credit, all the rest of your band would want it too. I can't give credit to them all. I do not know them as well as I do you. But, I'll do this, Starblanket. If you will be responsible for them, I will give every one of your Indians credit. I only want to deal with one man, and that is Starblanket. Call up your men and have a talk with them. You are the Chief, and what you tell your Indians to do, they ought to do, especially now, when you need provisions and I am willing to help you."

He asked me what I wanted him to do. I repeated that he would have to be responsible to me for the debts of all the Indians in his band. I told him that when the treaty time came he would have to call his men (he would know the amount each Indian owed me) and collect the money to pay me. He agreed. I told him to talk to his men, and that I would listen to the meeting. I was a hard fox to catch.

Starblanket called his men to a meeting, and then each man told me what he wanted. I figured that the amount of the orders came to seven hundred and seventy-five dollars. I told Starblanket that since it was late, I would give out the goods in the morning. He was pleased.

I didn't sleep much that night. I kept thinking about what a risk I was taking in giving that much money or goods on credit to a band of Indians. The next morning I gave each Indian the supplies that he wanted. I figured up the exact amount. It came to seven hundred and eighty-nine dollars.

Starblanket said, "You are well acquainted with Captain Macdonald (he was the man who would pay the treaty money). When treaty time comes around, try to get him to pay my band first."

He was no fool, that Starblanket! I went back to Lebret. When my wife found out what I had done, she was worried. She thought I had thrown the money away. I told her that she must have faith in the Indians; that the money was safe.

On the fifth of August, Starblanket rode up to my door. He said he had just got word, riding through Fort Qu'Appelle, that treaty money would be paid at the Fort on the seventh of August. (I had known this for two days.) He had come to see me, he said, to get a little tea, sugar, and tobacco, so that he could call his men, remind them of their promises, and advise them to pay me. I gave him tea, sugar, tobacco, and some flour to make bannock for themselves.

I told him that I would be up to visit him at his camp the next day. There were six or seven hundred lodges of Indians camped on the flats around the Fort. They almost covered the flats between the two lakes, Mission and Echo.

I should mention that when Starblanket had wanted me to give him credit, I had told him that I would have to charge him a little more for the goods than if I were trading. This was because I was taking a great risk, and I would have to charge a little interest.

When I rode up to Starblanket's lodges, they were glad to see me. The old women began to sing in Cree that this was the man that had given them credit when they had been near the Milk River. I will explain Starblanket's idea of wanting to be the first man paid.

He had said, "If I don't get paid first, it is going to be hard on me. There are a great many traders here. If other bands are paid first, my men will see them trading and will want to trade too."

I told him that I would influence Captain MacDonald. This was on the sixth, and the Indians were to be paid next day. I asked MacDonald this favor on the sixth.

He answered, "Welsh, I owe you several favors, but my interpreter may not be along very early in the morning."

I asked him what time he was going to commence paying the treaty money. He said at ten o'clock. I told him I would do the interpreting for him until his man came along. He was delighted. I fixed that all right!

I went to Starblanket's tent, and told him that in the morning when he saw my horse tied at the tent of Captain MacDonald he should rush his Indians in. He did. We had all Starblanket's band paid off by two o'clock in the afternoon. Then the interpreter came and took my place. MacDonald wanted me to stay for the rest of the day, but I had business to attend to. I had to watch my Indians.

About five o'clock I heard my name called in Cree. It was Starblanket's voice. He wanted me to come to his tent. I felt a little uncertain about things, and wondered whether or not I was going to make a success of my transaction.

I went over to the door of Starblanket's tent. They all said to come in, come in. They had made a fine seat purposely for me near the middle and back of the tent. It was covered with a clean Hudson's Bay blanket, and fine skins. They invited me to sit down. They offered me a cup of tea in a big flowered blue cup. The traders, I myself, used to sell those cups for twenty-five cents a pair. I took the tea. It was well sweetened and very nice. I enjoyed drinking tea with my Indians.

After I had taken my tea, Starblanket came, stood in front of me, and paid me his bill. I was sitting down. He asked me to count the money. His bill was correct. He paid me in full.

Starblanket's men were sitting around his tent. There were about thirty men. There were about thirty old women also. Starblanket told his men to come along, one at a time, and pay his bill. Everyone paid me. I didn't lose a cent on the transaction.

I had a big boodle of money now. I asked Starblanket to come and see me at my place the next day. I had a little horse, a buffalo runner, that he had often wished to own, so when he came to my place the next day, I asked him if he had a common horse that was worth about twenty dollars. He said he had one with him, and asked me to go and look at him.

I told him that if he would give me this horse he could have my buffalo runner. He almost fell on his knees he was so proud. I traded with Starblanket for a great many years after that. He died in 1927, or 1928.

Starblanket was a very good man if you knew how to take him, but if you didn't he was a hard nut to crack. I mean that he had a mind of his own. When he said a thing he meant it, and he always kept his word.

About two years after this transaction, Starblanket took up his Reserve north-east of the Fort. He began to work on it, but was dissatisfied, and disappointed. The Indian Department promised him assistance, and then didn't keep its promises. He was very unhappy because his freedom had been taken from him. He wanted to live his life as he had always lived it, roaming on the prairie with the wild buffalo.

He would not consent to send his children to school. He wouldn't listen to anybody, the Agent, or even the Commissioner. He came to me. I told him that he might be making a mistake. I told him also that I had been moving about on the plains and hadn't been able to send my children to school, but now I was starting to get them educated. Then I asked him if it wouldn't be wise for him to get his children educated too, so that they would be able to read and put things down in writing as mine would be able to do. Anyway I told him that he had better send his children to school willingly, otherwise the authorities would come to his tent and take them.

He said he hadn't thought of that. Then he said that he would send them for my sake, but he wouldn't send them for the Agent or anybody else.

I told him to go home and think it over, that there was plenty of time. I also told him that the Archbishop Langevin was coming from Fort Garry with a big crowd of people, that they would visit all the Indian Reserves, and that I wanted him to act like the man that he always was. I said I would go often and give him advice, tell him how to act when the Archbishop arrived. And so I did.

A few days before the Archbishop arrived, I went out to see Starblanket, and told him what time the Archbishop would arrive. I asked him if he were still willing to let his children go to school and listen to Father Hugonard's advice. He replied that he would let them go for me, but for nobody else.

The Archbishop's party arrived. The Indians received rations from the Government, and held a big pow-wow at the File Hills Reserve. A man named McNeil was in charge of this reserve.

McNeil took Starblanket to the Bishop and said, "This is Chief Starblanket. He has promised to send his children to school."

"I never promised you to send my children. You are a liar," Starblanket answered. Then Father Hugonard spoke up. He told Starblanket that he had promised to let his children go to school. Starblanket answered Father Hugonard as he had McNeil.

I had explained to the Archbishop beforehand that Starblanket would not take orders from Father Hugonard, the Agent, the Bishop or anybody else, but because we had been friends on the plains, he had promised me to send his children to the white man's school.

The Bishop asked to have me called to speak to

Starblanket. When I came he said, "Welsh, go and stand beside the Agent, and explain to him what Starblanket agreed to do for you."

I did. I explained to the Agent, to the Bishop and to the whole crowd just how Starblanket felt. Father Hugonard asked Starblanket if what I had said was true. He replied that it was. But he said what the others had said was not true, that he had not made, nor would he make them any promises.

The next morning it was stated in the paper published at Fort Qu'Appelle that the Indian Agent had persuaded Starblanket to send his children to school.

I liked Starblanket. He was eighty years of age when he died. I missed him.

Starblanket was one of the last Chiefs to come into the Fort Qu'Appelle Treaty. He was a man of strong opinions. You could not easily sway him. He was always against Father Hugonard who tried to boss him. One afternoon he came to my place at Lebret all dressed up and painted for war. He was camped with his people at the top of the hill to the east of Lebret, where the Canadian National Railway turns into the coulee to Balcarres. He was going to rebel against Father Hugonard and General Middleton. He had ammunition which he had bought from Antoine LaRocque. LaRocque was not aware that orders had gone out not to sell ammunition to the Indians. He was arrested for this and I had to pay part of his fine. But he repaid me later.

The trouble with Riel was going on at that time. And of course the sympathies of Starblanket and his people were with Riel. Middleton was on his way to Batoche (1885). He was nervous about Starblanket so he sent a detachment of fifty or sixty of his men to Starblanket's reserve at the File Hills to see what was going on. The sergeant in charge of the soldiers tried to explain things to Starblanket, but the Chief was such an irritable character that, as soon as they left his Reserve, he gave orders to his men to lift camp and move to a suitable fighting place.

Starblanket never made any decisions in any of his dealings with white people without consulting me. So he said to his people, "I will talk with Wa-Ka-Koot-Chick. Come with me, my headman and my three principal wives, and I will talk over what I am going to do with this Shee-maw-kanish O-kee-maw, and this white medicine man (Father Hugonard) who wants all our children."

It was early afternoon when they came to my place. Starblanket brought a pitcher of brandy to my wife. I always kept this pitcher as a little souvenir of my old friend. The Chief was very fond of my wife. He used to call her "Ne-dan-che." That was Cree for daughter. It was a name not lightly given. It was a great honor from a Chief. Of course she always made a big fuss over him, and put on a feast. In those days in the buffalo country, Chief Starblanket was somebody. And no one denied that, except some of the Indian agents who tried to make very big fellows of themselves because they had been given a little authority over the Indians. They thought their *little* jobs very important. They were too green to see that if Chief Starblanket wanted to start a fuss—they would all be scalped in their beds. The Hudson's Bay Company was not like that. They treated the Indians with respect. Of course they had been trading with them for a long, long time. They knew how to handle them. And as well, even if they always did get the best of the bargain in trading, they treated them with ceremony, and as if they had some brains.

On this day Starblanket said to me, "You know that Riel means business. He wants to take this country for his people, and the Indians. We would be better off. You see what white man's rule is doing? We are going to wipe out Father Hugonard. My people are bitter." He asked my opinion.

"Why don't you," he said, "join the rebellion? Riel is of your people. You have cause to rebel. I have come to ask you that. I want to tell you how we feel against Father Hugonard and to ask your advice. I want to know what you think. And as well, there is Shee-maw-kanish O-kee-maw (General Middleton) who is against my people."

I said to Starblanket, as I said to everyone, "I have had my rights. I am satisfied. I will have nothing to do with Riel. I sold my scrip. I got what I wanted. You must not join Riel. You must quit this rebellion, too, against Father Hugonard. he wants to do what is best for your people. But he is a little impatient. My friend, you must see that this fellow Riel will only get you and your people into trouble. I will tell you what I will do. I will hitch up my runner and we will go to the fort and have a talk with General Middleton, who is there, and the Chief Factor, Archibald Macdonald, at the Hudson's Bay Company. We will fix up a peace. You will agree with what the Chief Factor and I tell you, because you know what we say will be the best for you and your children. Haven't you confidence in us? We will tell you what is the right thing. That will be to sign a peace. You must agree not to take up arms. How is that?"

He said, "That is good advice. I will agree to whatever you and the Hudson's Bay Company say. But I will not come to-day. Shee-maw-kanish has got to come and see me."

So I said, "I will take Father Hugonard and George Fisher with me to the Fort and make arrangements with Shee-maw-kanish O-kee-maw (General Middleton) to meet you at George Fisher's house to-morrow to talk this business over. How will that do? If you come, I will guarantee that no harm will come to you." He agreed.

Next day Starblanket arrived. A message was sent to General Middleton that everything was ready. I would bring Starblanket and Father Hugonard to meet him at George Fisher's place, I said. Fisher's place is on the Mission Lake between Lebret and Fort Qu'Appelle. Some people by the name of Evans live in this house now.

"Come," I said, "we will get this over."

We left his three wives at my place. Two of them were sisters, and they never had so much as one fight. But then Indian women did not fight over their husbands. My wife said she would get a fine supper for us, and that we should not be too late.

I drove up to the door where Starblanket waited. There

was no humility in that man. I can see him yet. He stood on the steps of my house. He was very proud. Then he threw his blanket half across his shoulder, and stepped down and into my cutter.

Before Starblanket had left his camp, he had posted his warriors within gunshot distance at intervals, so that if anything went wrong they could rush down and rescue their Chief.

Starblanket and Middleton faced each other. Middleton presented his hand, but Starblanket refused it saying that he would not take the White Chief's hand in friendship until they had made peace.

Middleton asked him, "Will you go back to your Reserve and do your work and keep quiet?"

Starblanket answered, "That was what we were doing when your men came and troubled us. I am no man to be frightened. The first one of your men that comes on my reserve will be shot."

Middleton said he was not looking for trouble and if Starblanket would go back and remain quiet there would be none. Starblanket agreed to go back only on that condition. Now Starblanket shook hands with General Middleton and everything was over. They had made peace.

There must be some record of this meeting either in the books of the Hudson's Bay Company, or in the records of General Middleton. Poor Starblanket! He would always do the right thing.

When we got back to my house, my wife had a very special supper. She had made des boulettes, la poutine dans le sac, et de croxegnols, or des beignes. The boulettes were small meat balls made of buffalo meat, tallow, salt, pepper and a little onion all chopped together with a small axe which the Crees call pa-ka-men-nam, and made into little balls rolled in flour, and boiled with potatoes with a very little water. That was a fine dish! This was something the Chief liked.

The poutine dans le sac was what you call a suet pudding. It was a great favorite with the traders. It was made of flour, fine buffalo tallow, those big raisins we carried in trade, and nutmeg. This dough was put in a bag and boiled. In those days we served it with a sauce laced, as we used to say, with brandy. The real stuff.

But de croxegnols. There was something! We made that always for the New Year's celebrations, and on special occasions only. It was a dough mixture. Flour and fine tallow mixed with water. First the dough was rolled smooth, then cut in squares. Then each square was slit into five divisions, like fingers, and these fingers were twisted into fancy shapes, all criss-crossed. Then these were thrown into boiling fat. Some of them were very funny looking shapes when they were cooked, and they appealed to the fancy of the Indians. Many the good buffalo robe I was able to buy at a right price after my Indians had had a good feed on my wife's de croxegnols! De croxegnols were something very special. I remember that, out on the plains on New Year's eve, the children used to get on top of the traders' houses and run long sharp sticks down the chimneys and spear the fine brown croxegnols out of the pots of boiling fat. They did this once to my wife, and what a surprise she got, when she saw that her fine brown croxegnols had disappeared. She was beginning to believe that spirits were around the place.

To get back to Starblanket. "My friend," I said to him, "We will now sit down to this feast." Always in those days, we gave the Chief the place of honor when we made a feast for him. "Sit at the head of the table," I told him. I sat at his right hand. His wives sat on either side of him. I said grace. Starblanket and his wives clasped their hands and bowed their heads. Now we ate our meal. Not a word was spoken. The Indians eat in complete silence. We always observed the Indian customs. This was their way of giving thanks to their Manitou. When the meal was finished, I said grace again. That was the conclusion of the peace that Starblanket had agreed to keep with the white queen. I thought a great deal of Starblanket. As I have said elsewhere, we were like brothers. He was a reasonable man.

CHAPTER FIFTEEN

I Build a House in Style

I passed the winter of 1877-78 at Lebret. This was after the signing of the Qu'Appelle treaty, and after the Indians had been placed on Reserves. I told my wife that since we were going to stay, I was going to build a house. I took my axe, went up the hill, and began to chop poplar logs. In three days I had chopped three hundred logs twenty feet long. I could not haul my logs on jumpers, for there was no snow, so I made five travois to haul them on.

Early one morning I hitched my horses to the travois, and made two trips a day. I got down twenty logs a day. I was alone, only myself and my horses. But I had one horse that would do just what I wanted him to. He was as good as a man. I would put him on the trail, and when I told him to go, he would lead the other horses down the hill and stop where I was piling the logs. His name was Piegan. He came from the Indian Nation of that name.

After my logs were drawn, I had a man hew them on two sides to flatten them. Then I had him pick out the best logs and put up a house twenty feet square. When he got it finished, the wall was twelve feet high, dove-tailed at the corners.

Now I wanted to finish the house with good wood. The carpenter, who was a good one, advised me to let the log frame dry for a couple of months before doing any more. He said I would gain by it. I took his advice.

At the end of two months I got the carpenter to come back

and finish the roof. There were no shingles to be had here at that time. Hewed timber was used instead, and covered with boards. The carpenter finished my house this way, and made a peaked roof. Everybody began to think and say that I was putting up a swell house.

I decided to use lumber for a floor if I could get it. The carpenter said that he knew of only one man, Father Hugonard, who had lumber to sell, and it was poor. This was during the late summer, and I would have to go to Fort Garry for my winter supplies.

I went to Father Hugonard and asked him to let me see his lumber. I didn't know much about lumber, but I thought that this, which was whip-sawed, was very rough. I asked Father Hugonard how long and how wide the boards were, and how much he wanted for each. He replied that they were ten feet long and four inches wide, and that the price was twenty-five cents a piece.

"Twenty-five cents a piece!" I exclaimed.

Father Hugonard told me that he was offering it to me cheap, that he was doing me a favor to sell at this price.

"Look here, Father," I said, "I won't buy your lumber. If you call twenty-five cents a board cheap, I don't. I thought you were here to set a good example to people. I will get better lumber than you have ever seen."

He asked me where I would get it. I told him in Fort Garry. He said, "Hah! How will you draw it?"

I told him that I had lots of horses and quite a bit of money.

Well, nobody could do me, so I took ten carts and an extra team of horses and started for Fort Garry. When I got to Fort Garry, I bought a waggon and a double harness. I had never had a waggon or a harness before. At that time waggons and harnesses were very cheap in Fort Garry. I only paid sixty dollars for the outfit.

Then I hitched two of my best horses in the waggon and drove down to the lumber yard. I went to the office and met the man in charge. His name was McCall. He said that he had never seen me before, and asked me where I hailed from.

I told him that my name was Norbert Welsh, that I had come from Fort Qu'Appelle, and wanted lumber. He struck his hands together and said, "That far to draw lumber!" Then he added, "Welsh, do you see that lumber yard? Go and pick your lumber. I won't go with you. Satisfy yourself. Take as many boards as you want for your building, and when you are done loading bring your team to the office door. I'll measure it and see if you have the right amount for your house." So I did.

He had given me a rough estimate of the amount of lumber to take, and when he measured it he found that I had four boards too many. The lumber was sixteen feet long and six inches wide, tongued and grooved. McCall said that since I had come so far for the lumber he would make me a present of the extra four boards.

I pulled out a roll of bills to pay him. When he saw the size of my roll he said, "My God! You have plenty of money."

I paid him. I just forget the amount. I think it was twenty-two dollars. This lumber cost me just half as much as if I had bought it from Father Hugonard.

On top of the boards I piled five sacks of bacon and some flour, seventy one hundred pound sacks. Then I took a bull-hide (buffalo) and laced it over the flour so that if it rained my provisions would not get wet. I bought a cutter and placed it on top of this. Then I bought a plow, a set of harrows, and whippletrees, put them on top of the load, and laced them on well. I laced them so well that I didn't have to touch them until I got home. Well, that waggon was the first waggon (it was called a Chatham waggon) to come to Fort Qu'Appelle. That was nearly sixty years ago.

Besides this waggon I had five carts loaded with flour, one thousand pounds apiece; one cart was loaded with tea, sugar, tobacco, and other stuff; one was loaded with doors, glasses (panes for windows), paint, and nails; one with all kinds of merchandise, prints, calicoes, and another was loaded with bedsteads, chairs, and clapboards.

I made the round trip in thirty days. I drew that lumber three hundred and thirty-five miles. Nobody before or after that brought lumber to Fort Qu'Appelle on a waggon. After that it came by the railroad: by the Canadian Pacific Railway to Qu'Appelle, and it was drawn the twenty miles from there.

When the people at the Fort saw me coming with all that lumber and goods they were surprised. They were coming from far and near to see my waggon. When Father Hugonard saw me bring that lumber he said, "Welsh, you are a hard nut to crack."

I told him that when Norbert Welsh made up his mind to do a thing he was going to do it.

When the house was finished we moved into it. My wife told me that we had made one mistake, that I had not made any provision for a kitchen, that the house was too small. I had not thought of it, because we had been used to a wintering house with two bedrooms, and one big room for a kitchen. I told her that I would soon get a kitchen built on to the house.

I had a man working for me who was a rough carpenter. I told him to go to work and build a kitchen for me as fast as he could. He could have another man to help, I told him. I planned a big kitchen, fourteen by twenty feet. We had lots of children and I wanted my wife to have lots of room. Batiste said that the only thing that would delay him would be the lumber for the floor.

"Ho!" I said, "I'll hitch up that fine team of mine and drive down to Birtle, Manitoba. It is only one hundred and forty-five miles. If I am not back on the fourth day, I will be back on the fifth."

I knew those horses of mine could travel. I got to Birtle in two days. On the evening of the second day I got my lumber loaded on the waggon. On the morning of the third day, I started for home. I reached home on the evening of the third day just at supper time.

When the kitchen was finished, we lathed it with willows,

and plastered it with mud mixed with water. When the walls were dry, we white-washed them with lime. We put the cooking-stove up. Now the house was finished.

I didn't go out after buffalo that winter. There was no use. There was now only a small drove to be seen here and there on the plains. But I was busy. I had lots of goods and did a lot of trading. I cut and drew rails too, that winter.

CHAPTER SIXTEEN

I Turn to Farming

The North-West was turning into a white man's country. The buffalo were scarce, about gone you might say. The Government was shutting the Indians up on Reserves, and everything was getting rather tame. In the North-West the Indians were beginning to be well civilized. The Chiefs were fine men. Take One Arrow, Poundmaker, Starblanket, all signers of the treaties, they were fine, intelligent men. They could rule their bands.

Of course the bands fought with other tribes, but that was for hunting territory—expansion you might say; white men do the same—but they didn't trouble white men. I remember once being chased by Indians. It was in the States. I was with a fur brigade from Fort Gary to St. Paul. William Rhone, the man I was with, went on a spree at St. Cloud and kept it up for a week. The rest of the brigade—there were A.G.B. Bannatyne, Robbie Tait, William Logan, Sandy Logan, Patterson, Barber, Andrew McDermott, Junior—went on and left me to bring Rhone.

I caught up to the brigade at a place called Black Sand Hills near Red Lake, Minnesota. Rhone was still drunk, but I had him in the waggon. I found the others all drunk, just sobering up a little. Well, I had had nothing to eat for a day and a night, so I hurried and began to cook breakfast. I told the boy, Joe Ledaux, that we would have a good breakfast, since we were with a band of drunkards and would have to look after them. All that I had had to eat in two days was a box of soda biscuits. When breakfast was ready, I called all our men, and we all had a good breakfast.

For some reason, while we were eating, I felt uneasy. The thought of these half-drunken men bothered me. It was raining a little. After breakfast I asked Ledaux to wash the dishes and put away everything, while I attended to the horses. I wanted to get these men on the trail, travelling, right away.

I threw my saddle and bridle on my back and started on a run for the horses. I crossed the valley, got hold of my horse, saddled and bridled him, and jumped on his back. I looked behind. Over the big hill, which is now called Leaf City, I saw something coming on the run. For a moment I thought it was deer; then I saw that it was Indians—a war-party.

I tell you I galloped those horses into camp at full race. I called out to the men, "Get up, you drunken beggars. There's a war-party after us!"

They moved fast. You would never have thought they were half drunk. I don't think it took us more than five minutes to get ready and skip. It was a good thing for us that the war-party was on foot and that we had our carts. We raced at full speed and had almost reached Red Lake, a distance of five miles, when three of their runners overtook us.

There were about sixty Indians in this war-party including the Chief, who wore a big red Hudson's Bay blanket. One of them caught hold of McDermott's horse, and told us to stop. He said that the Chief wanted to have a talk with us.

McDermott pulled out his gun, and told the Indian to let the horse go or he would shoot him. The Indians were well armed. There were ten of us, but we had only four guns. We could not put up a very good fight, especially the fellows who had been having one devil of a time ("making whoopee!").

I had my double-barrelled gun in my hand. It was loaded. Beside my cart there was a great big fellow, a brave, all vermilioned and with yellow stripes running down his body. They were painted for war, you see. I kept close watch over him. I did not want to shoot unless I had to.

Well, the upshot of it was that McDermott's horse knocked the Indian away from his bridle, and down. We raced our horses into the river and made them swim the carts, and thus managed to get across the Red Lake River and away from them. Patterson got out a big plug of tobacco. He was still drunk and wanted to give it to the Indians—to ask them to come across the river for it.

We stopped for nothing, but travelled all that day and night. We were afraid they might follow, attack, and rob us. I tell you that race sobered my men up fine. They were okay now.

Those Indians were from the Red Lake country, and although they were on a war-party, I don't think they would have killed us. As a rule they would not harm white men, but at that time they thought nothing of robbing a trader or a traveller—taking his clothes—and turning him loose, naked. For my part, I would sooner be shot than stripped.

That fall, after my deal with Starblanket, I went to Fort Garry and got a thousand dollars worth of goods, the same kind of goods we always carried. We called it trading goods. There was nothing fancy, no silk or lace, just ordinary trading goods.

There was no more hunting on the plains. The buffalo were gone. The Indians and half-breeds came to my house to trade, but business was very poor. Trading in furs was practically at an end. There was just a stray buffalo robe, and wolf, coyote, fox, or other small skins. I began to buy cattle. I bought five cows.

In the spring of 1878 I began to farm. I put in two acres of wheat, four acres of oats, two bushels of barley, half an acre of potatoes, and half an acre of peas.

That fall when I threshed, I got a hundred bushels of wheat, two hundred and forty bushels of oats, a hundred and twenty bushels of barley, and over two hundred bushels of potatoes. The peas, I had let the people pick green.

I sold a hundred bushels of potatoes to the North-West Mounted Police at Fort Qu'Appelle for two dollars and a half a bushel; a hundred and fifty bushels of oats for two dollars a bushel, to Captain French of the Mounted Police—he was later shot in the rebellion—who was taking a homestead; a hundred and twenty bushels of barley for two dollars and a half a bushel; fifty bushels of wheat, for seed wheat, at three dollars and a half a bushel.

Father Hugonard and I were the first two farmers at Fort Qu'Appelle. Later, in the year 1879, I brought in the first harvester. It was shipped on the steamboat from Fort Garry to Fort Ellice, and I brought it from there on my cart. To-day a binder is used instead of a harvester. The harvester only cut the wheat and threw it in sheaves, which we tied by hand.

This same year when the Indian treaty money was paid, I rigged up four carts and went from one Reserve to another, where the Agent was paying the Indians, and traded. I took in from transactions with Indians at these treaties a little over a thousand dollars in cash, but no buffalo robes.

I missed my trading life on the plains. They had been busy years, but encouraging years. At every turn I had made money. It was a pity I couldn't keep it. If I had my sight, I could make money again. Sometimes when I can't sleep, I take a little run around my life as a trader, from where I began to where I left off, and I have a very good time.[1]

In the spring when I had put in my wheat, my neighbor, Joe Poitras, a hunter, put in some wheat too. He planted his on the fifteenth of April because he thought that wheat had to be put in early to avoid frosts. I let him go on. He was twenty days ahead of me. I cut his wheat and mine on the same day with my harvester.

There is a little secret in how I got ahead of my neighbor. Long ago, near Fort Garry there were a lot of farmers along the Red River. They were rich farmers, although they had small farms. I had worked for one of them. His name was Walter Burke. He was the son of an Irish father and a Sioux mother. When he wanted to sow his wheat, we drew water in pails from the Red River on yokes slung from our shoulders,

1. Norbert Welsh was, in 1931, eighty-seven years of age, and blind.

and we filled barrels. Then we put lime, the size of my fist, into each barrel, put the wheat into the barrels and let it soak all night. The next morning we drained the wheat, let it dry a little, then sowed it. In three days the wheat was up. It was clean wheat. No smut, no rust.

In 1880 the surveyors came out to survey the country. Bill Thompson was the head man. He had a big outfit. He asked me if I would do his freighting. I agreed. First I rigged up ten carts and went down to Fort Ellice to get his supplies, which he had brought to that post on the steamboat.

He had a big shipment of supplies there. Tea, sugar, bacon, flour, a forty-gallon barrel of syrup—his summer's supplies. I delivered his freight to the Hudson's Bay post at Fort Qu'Appelle.

When I delivered his goods, Thompson asked me if, when he wanted supplies, I would deliver them to wherever he was working. He said that he would send a map with his letters to show me exactly where to go. I agreed.

I kept delivering his stuff to him as he wanted it. We got on fine together. Fall came and Thompson had to stop surveying. About the end of October he came to my house on the flats of Lebret, and camped there one night. He paid me the balance of what he owed me for freighting. When everything was calculated there was sixteen hundred dollars and seventy-five cents coming to me. He said that he would have to give me a cheque, and, since I was going to Fort Garry, I could get it cashed there. At that time there was no bank west of Portage-la-Prairie.

Thompson asked me if I could let him have a bushel of potatoes to have to eat on the way to Fort Garry. I told my boy to go and fetch thirty potatoes. Thompson asked, why thirty potatoes. They would make a bushel, I told him. He laughed and said I was crazy. I told the boy to fetch them, and to take them just as they came. He did.

We weighed the potatoes. They weighed sixty-one and a half pounds. I told Thompson that I would make him a present of the one and a half pounds extra.

That's how the place—the valley of the Qu'Appelle—got such a big name for farming. Thompson went to Winnipeg and reported that the country, the Qu'Appelle valley, was by what he had seen, the garden of the North-West. That's one thing that helped rush the people to the North-West.

Thompson started for Winnipeg. A week later I started, and overtook him at Brandon. We met the Canadian Pacific Railway there; construction had been delayed for the winter. I left my man and horses at Brandon and took the train to Winnipeg with Thompson. That was the first ride I had on the first railroad that was built in the North-West.

When we got to Winnipeg, Thompson paid me in cash—I had not accepted his cheque since we had planned to meet in Winnipeg—and I bought some stuff that I wanted.

I bought a buckboard, the first one that was brought out here, thirty ninety-eight pound sacks of flour, and I also bought a lot of other stuff, tea, sugar, bacon, tobacco—my own supplies for the winter. I always had men working for me, and then I could always sell stuff. I paid for everything I bought, and had six hundred dollars left over. I kept three hundred dollars, and put three hundred dollars in the Merchants Bank, Winnipeg. This was my first bank account.

I shipped my stuff by train to Brandon. The day of the Red River cart was over. I got on the train. A big blizzard came, and at High Bluffs we got stuck in a snow drift and were held up there for three days and three nights.

About three o'clock on the third day, sixteen bobsleighs arrived from Portage-la-Prairie to get the passengers. Every sleigh was crowded with passengers; men, women, and children. We waited there for two days until the train got through.

When we got to Brandon, I was surprised to see Thompson's brother John, who had worked with his brother as assistant surveyor. I asked him what he was doing there. He said he was taking an outfit to the West, and that he had a letter for me from his brother. Billy told me in the letter that he was sending an outfit to the West with his brother, and asked me to keep an eye on him on account of the horses and things.

I told John Thompson that I had seven sleighs, jumpers, and toboggans to look after, without looking after another outfit. The reason I said this was because his horses were poor, and my horses were fat. I knew that these poor horses could not keep up with mine.

But on the other hand, I was kind of stuck. I had tried to hire a man to come back with me, but couldn't find one. I had a big outfit to handle alone, especially in the winter time.

I loaded up. I fixed everything right, lashed my load well, fixed it solid. When the load was properly lashed it made it much easier for the horses to travel. It prevented the goods from slipping from side to side.

Thompson and his men were greenhorns. They didn't know how to pack their loads. I tried to help them, but when I wanted to put a thing here, they wanted to put it there. So I let them alone. I thought, "If you know better than I, go ahead."

The first night we camped—it was late now, the beginning of December—everybody brought in his bed-clothes except Thompson. I always carried a single feather tick. I was fussy about sleeping with other people, and so I always carried a single bed. Thompson wanted to sleep with me. I told him there was no room, but finally I agreed to let him sleep with me for one night.

I went to bed, and to sleep. I awoke to hear Thompson telling his men, "We have Welsh cornered, for he can't get along alone. We'll make him put his big horses onto our loads, and we'll put our lighter horses onto his."

I listened to that. I did not say anything, but I thought to myself, "If that's the kind of men you are, I'll leave you right here to-morrow morning." Thompson came to bed. He had me crowded out and the bed to himself most of the night.

In the morning, after breakfast, Thompson ordered his men to put some of their things on top of my load. When I told him that I would not allow him to do that, he asked what

I could do about it, since I was alone. He would see for himself in fifteen minutes, I told him.

I tied up my bed-clothes and feather tick in a rubber sheet, and loaded my stuff on my jumpers. I wasn't alone, but Thompson did not know that. I had my man Piegan (my horse) with me. I got my horses and hitched them up. Although there was a lot of snow, the grass showed through and marked the trail. I put my horse, Piegan, on the trail and started him. I put the other six horses, one after the other, on the trail to follow him. When I got all my horses on their way, I cracked my whip, called goodbye to Thompson, started my horses to trot, and away I went.

Thompson and his men were helpless. He had six sleighs, and five men including himself. He and his men had started to get ready when I did, but before they were nearly ready I was gone.

As I had eaten a big breakfast, I decided not to stop for dinner. I made up my mind to put in a big day and to leave Thompson far behind. I must have travelled twenty-five miles that day. Thompson, I knew, would not be able to make more than fifteen.

I travelled until it got dark, and I had reached some bush where there was dry wood. It was well sheltered, so I un-hitched and hobbled my horses by their hind feet so they could paw with their forefeet through the snow and get grass. Then I built a big fire. All I had to do was to fry bacon or beef. When my kettle boiled, I went to get my grub.

Now I had made quite a few bannocks the day before so I would have enough for two or three days. When I lifted my bag of grub it seemed very light. I opened it. There was just one bannock left.

I had perceived, in the morning when I was packing up, that someone had tried to open, with an axe, a little trunk in which I carried merchandise, and a small keg of rum.

I was very hungry. I took my axe and chopped off a chunk of beefsteak to fry with bacon. I ate my supper and my last bannock. After supper I made six bannocks. To-day people would say that was a hard life. It was fine fun. I mixed my bannock outside in a big pan, you might say in the snow. Six bannocks would last me for three days.

Now what about my bed and tent? Well, I had a high jumper with high railings around the top. It was loaded with flour, but there was quite a space between the flour and the top of the railing. I decided to put my bed on top of the flour to save time spreading the tent. Then I spread the tent over the railings. I crawled under the covering and slept soundly that night.

I got up at five o'clock. My horses were eating, near-by. I took my soap and towel and washed my face in the snow. Then I made a fire and put on my tea-kettle. While I waited for it to boil, I cooked bacon and beef. I also put a bannock on a stick and planted it before the fire to toast. After a good breakfast, I felt as happy as a king.

Now I packed up my things and got my horses hitched up. Piegan was of course the first on the road. I never carried a watch, but I don't think it took me more than an hour to hitch up all my horses. There was no sign of Thompson. I had left him far behind. "Now," I said, "for another good day's work." (I used to talk to myself when I was travelling alone.)

That day I stopped for dinner at noon. On the road again, I travelled until nearly dark. That's the way I travelled until I got back to Lebret. I was ten days on the road. No man with me, just Piegan.

One day Piegan stopped, and I didn't know why. I cracked the whip. I yelled at him. He started, and stopped again. I commanded him again. He turned around and looked at me. I knew there was something wrong and ran towards him. I found that the shaggannappi, which went through the runner of the jumper and the end of the shaft, was broken. "Piegan," I told him, "you're a wise old horse." I fixed the shaggannappi; Piegan started, and away we went.

Thompson arrived at Lebret fifteen days after me. He was alive, and that was all. I liked Bill Thompson. He was still surveying in 1931. One couldn't meet a better man, but I didn't like his brother.

When Bill Thompson came back in the spring, he never spoke to me about having left his brother behind on the road, but he said that he would like to make an agreement with me. I asked him what it was. He said, "The way things are this is going to be the main point for surveys. There will be lots of surveying. I think it would be advisable for you and my brother to go into partnership and start a big store here."

"If that's what you want to talk about, Thompson, I may as well tell you now that I will have nothing to do with your brother," I replied.

Thompson did not ask me the reason, but I guess he knew what I thought of his brother. That's the reason I did not start a store with John Thompson.

CHAPTER SEVENTEEN

I Become a Freighter

For three years running I put in a crop. The third year wasn't a success. I had a patch of wheat, sixty acres, up on the hill north-west of Lebret. One couldn't wish for better wheat to look at. I got a man by the name of Tom Williams, brother of the late R.H. Williams of the Glasgow House, Regina, to cut and bind it for me. He charged me seventy-five cents an acre for cutting and binding it. The grain was so good that I would not use the harvester to cut it.

After the wheat had stood for eight days, I told my man that it must be dry, and that we would go and stack it. We started off from the valley and drove up the hill and to the farm. When we got near the wheat-field I said to my man, "That wheat looks very black." I jumped off the waggon, went to the wheat, picked a handful of heads, and rubbed them between my hands. The wheat was frozen.

This was about the last of July or the first of August. Apparently there had been a frost up on the plains that we hadn't noticed down in the valley. Then rainy weather had set in and had kept the grain heads up and full. I said, "To blazes with farming! I won't farm any more around here. That is too much money to throw away."

All the crops had frozen that year. In my transactions, breaking, farming, and machinery, I had spent three thousand dollars of my good buffalo money—and thrown it away on farming.

That winter, Captain Jaffray, head of the Mounted Police

126

stationed at Fort Qu'Appelle—he had a store beside the barracks—told me that flour was very scarce and expensive, and asked if I would haul some flour for him from Shoal Lake, Manitoba. That was nearly two hundred miles from the fort.

It was winter now, the beginning of January; there was nearly a foot of snow on the ground, and it was the time for blizzards. I asked Captain Jaffray how much flour he wanted hauled, and how much he would pay a sack, a hundred pound sack. He said he would like two hundred sacks, and asked how a dollar and a half a hundred would be.

"Oh, not at all, not at all. It will not do at all. Give me two dollars a sack and I will go and get it," I told him.

"That will make it very costly landed here, but I see that if I want to get the flour, I will have to give you your price. Anyway you're a pretty good fellow, Welsh," he answered.

So we agreed. I went home and figured the thing out. I figured that I could handle eighty sacks myself on my ten jumpers—a single horse to a jumper—and it would take fifteen jumpers to handle the remaining hundred and twenty sacks.

I went from house to house in Lebret, and asked the men if they could freight, and how many teams they could supply. I got the fifteen jumpers, and agreed to pay these freighters a dollar and seventy-five cents for each sack.

We rigged up and away we went. In all we had twenty-five jumpers. We got to Shoal Lake, where I had orders to get the flour from the grist mill. I got the two hundred sacks, and loaded up. It took me twenty days to make the round trip, that is to go and come.

That was a long distance to haul flour, but it was the nearest grist mill to Fort Qu'Appelle. Of course Father Hugonard had a little flour mill—I might say he had a pepper mill only a bigger style. It stood in a shed down where the church now stands on the flats at Lebret. Father Hugonard used to hitch a horse, an ox, or a team of horses to the mill and they would walk around and make it go.

Of course Father Hugonard hadn't any flour to sell. He just made a bagful now and then. Sometimes he would send a little of this flour around to his friends and neighbors. This flour was coarse, not sifted. You had to sift the bran out of it yourself. But it was good flour, good and strong. When you got a bannock made out of that flour it stayed with you just like pemmican.

Of course I did a lot of freighting after I stopped hunting buffalo, but I think another freighting trip that I made from Indian Head to Prince Albert is worth mentioning here.

It was the year after the Rebellion and I was here at Lebret. About the beginning of February, Jones, the Indian Agent from the Indian Head reserve, came and asked me where he could get freighters to haul flour from the Indian Head mill to Prince Albert. I told him that that was a long distance, that it was very cold, and that it would be difficult for the horses to get feed on the trail, because there was so much snow. I asked him how much he would pay a hundred to haul this flour.

He replied that he would pay three dollars a hundred pounds. I told him that if he would give me three dollars and a half a hundred, I would get his flour there. He said the Department wouldn't pay that much. I wouldn't take it for less, I told him. He made some further excuses, and finally he said that to make sure the flour got to Prince Albert—the Indian Department was sending it to the Indians up there—he supposed they would have to pay me my price.

At that I told him I wouldn't be responsible for damage to the sacks, because I would have to hire other freighters to help me. He asked me how soon I could be at Indian Head to start on the trip. "In three days," I told him.

There were three hundred sacks to be hauled. All I could handle myself was one hundred sacks. So I had to get other freighters, but that wasn't hard. There were plenty of freighters now. It was a hard winter and everybody needed money.

I went around and selected my freighters. I offered to pay them three dollars and twenty-five cents a hundred. They agreed. The next day we got ready and started for The Head. We packed the flour on our jumpers and set out on the trip. It took us twenty days to reach Prince Albert, a distance of about three hundred miles. We travelled through blizzards and there was deep snow, but we made good time. Nothing was destroyed.

When I delivered my flour to the farm instructor at Prince Albert, I told him we were short of grub, and that we were almost out of bacon. He asked how much I wanted. I wanted to know the price first, I told him. He replied that he would not sell, but he would give it to me because I had accommodated them by bringing the flour.

He gave me one hundred and fifty pounds of fine bacon and asked if that would be enough to do us until we got back to Lebret. I said that it would, and thanked him. Then I distributed the bacon among the men who needed it, but I kept the biggest part myself. Nothing but right, eh? It took us ten days to return to Lebret.

I had quite a time with my men that winter. None of them wanted to lead—to break the trail—they all wanted to spare their horses. The first man who started would naturally be the leader. On the way to Prince Albert, I had to lead most of the time. At five o'clock in the morning, I shouted, and all the freighters had to get up. On the return trip, though, I made some of the beggars lead. I even stopped a whole day in one place to force some one else to lead.

We carried canvas tents and camp stoves on these trips. After the snow was cleared off the ground, the tent was set up. If we could get dry slough hay or willows, we spread this on the ground for a bed. Each man carried for bedding, a buffalo robe, and one Hudson's Bay blanket (three point single blanket).

Fort Qu'Appelle was now quite a place. The back of the barracks of the North-West Mounted Police was up against the hill behind where the Golf Club house now stands. Some of the buildings were in the ravine for protection.

The Mounties were great about putting on horse races. Jaffray had a fine black horse. To see him you would think that he could jump over the moon. Well, one 24th of May, they decided to put on a horse race and clean up some prizes. They subscribed a hundred dollars among the officers and men. Each man gave so much. Some gave a whole month's pay. Bob Mackie of Fort Qu'Appelle still laughs about this race. He was in the force and subscribed a month's pay.

Well the officers and men of the force came along and shook the handful of bills in the face of the crowd gathered around the barracks, challenging them to bet.

Roderick Ross laughed, turned to me and said, "Welsh, take my horse and beat these fellows. I'll put up the hundred dollars."

He knew that I could ride. The other fellows hadn't seen me chase buffalo on fast runners. I said, "All right." Ross walked up to Jaffray and put up the hundred dollars. Captain Steele, afterward Major-General Steele,[1] was the keeper of the bet.

I put a bridle on the horse but no saddle. I walked and led my horse to the mound from which we were going to start the half-mile race. We mounted. A Mounted Policeman started us. "Go!" he said, and away we went.

Jaffray's horse was so spirited that I thought he was going to jump over me. I let him go. I kept holding my horse back. As we neared the end of the track, I let my horse creep up until he was neck and neck with the black, then I turned and called, "Goodbye" to the rider. I let my horse go, and finished fifty yards ahead of Jaffray's horse.

I tell you the Mounted Police were down-hearted that day. They prided themselves on having the finest horses and the most expert riders in the North-West. The pride of the Police in their horse and rider was crushed. Riding was nothing to me.

Ross collected the bet. He gave me five dollars in gold.

I think the last demonstration of riding we old buffalo hunters gave on the plains was at the time the Marquis of Lorne visited Fort Qu'Appelle in August of 1881. I organized a troop of about a hundred buffalo hunters who had settled around Lebret. We mounted our fast buffalo runners and rode up to the top of the hill on the south side of Lebret. When I saw the Royal party coming along the old Hudson's

---

1. General Steele in the Great War.

Bay trail on their way from Indian Head, I parted my troop, placing half on each side of the road to form a guard of honor. When the party came opposite us, we fired volley after volley into the air from our repeating rifles. The procession halted. The Marquis dismounted and came and shook hands with each one of us. We all mounted again, and again we sent a salute ringing through the air. Then, prancing, and galloping our runners, we escorted the party down the hill and into Lebret. There were big celebrations at both Lebret and Fort Qu'Appelle. Sitting Bull and his warriors attended this celebration. They had been camping in the valley for some time awaiting the arrival of the Governor-General of Canada. Sitting Bull wanted to apply for a reserve on Canadian territory. He claimed that a large area of the country extending southward to the States had formerly been an old hunting ground of the Sioux. He was quite right. He spoke to the Governor-General about it. He was no fool, that Sitting Bull. He believed in going to the headman with his requests. The old warrior came to see me at my place. He was very poor. I gave him some provisions for himself and his band. I had many good long chats with Sitting Bull.

Chapter Eighteen

An Indian Sun Dance

I went to a great many sun dances during the course of my travels. The last sun dance held on the plains was in charge of Chief Starblanket, File Hills Reserve. That was the last official Indian sun dance.[1] The Indian agent, John Wright, had to go away, so he asked me to keep an eye on the Indians. He was afraid the "boodlers," the whiskey traders, would sell liquor to the Indians and get them wild.

In order to explain how a sun dance is put on, I will suppose that I am the Chief of the sun dance lodge. I give orders to my men to go and select a place to get trees to make the sun dance lodge. I select three men for this work and each man carries a gun. They get on horseback and gallop through the bluffs to find a spot where there are water and good trees. When they find a suitable tree—I have given them orders to pick out a good big tree with lots of branches on the top—each man fires his gun three times.

Then my braves mount, and each with a woman, his wife or another woman on his horse, waits for the signal of the guns. It comes and they gallop into the bush where the cutters are at work, and begin to cut trees.

The three men I selected bring this big tree to the spot that I have picked out for the sun dance lodge. They bring it very carefully so as not to break the branches. I tell them now to dig a deep hole, put the tree into this hole, plant it and

1. This sun dance was held some years after the signing of the Qu'Appelle Treaty.

make it as solid as possible. This is the centre tree.

Then the braves, each with a pole tied to the tail of his horse with shaggannappi, gallop back to the centre tree. It is time to make my tent. At a distance of twenty-five feet from the middle tree, I plant poles all around in a circle. Next I instruct my men to lay the rafters. They lay them from the centre tree to the posts that have been planted.

I give orders to one of my men to climb the centre tree, and cut the branches off the top of that tree to make a nest for the Manitou, about fifteen feet from the ground. They make this nest where the rafters meet. The centre tree is twenty-five feet high.

Brush is piled over the rafters to form a roof. I have a fine roof. It will shelter the dancers and protect them from the sun. I get my Indians to cut more trees. These they plant all around the tent as close as they can. These trees make a wall in case of a wind storm, also a shade for the dancers.

Now the outside of the tent is finished. I must prepare the inside. I instruct my men to make a door, and from this door, straight to the back of the tent, run two partitions to form a passage. This will give me two rooms, one on each side of the passage.

The men place straight green willow posts, one at each side of the door, and one at each side of the back of the tent. Then they run scantlings between the posts. Along these scantlings, they stand the green willows as tightly as they can, making a firm wall about four feet high. Then they bend the tops of these willows across the passage and knit them together. When this is finished it looks like basket weaving. There is a lot of work to this.

Now I select my people for the dance. I select six young boys and six young girls and tell them that they have got to dance for four days and four nights without eating or drinking. If they are not willing to do this, they are not capable of becoming medicine men or women.

In those days when a sun dance started, there were always plenty of white men there, hundreds of them. Everybody that travelled through the country went to see the sun dances. I collect from them. I expect to collect one dollar in money or goods from each person. If he does not pay, I will not allow him to enter the tent to see the dance. I call the dancers and give them a good drink of tea and a good meal. It is time to start the dance.

I divide my dancers. I put the six boys in one room and the six girls in the other. Their heads reach above the wall. They are well dressed and painted. I give them the war-whoop. They start to dance.

The girls have little green willow whistles in their mouths. They whistle softly as they begin to dance. They throw their bodies in a regular rhythm, bending from the knees. The boys, too, begin to dance and whistle. There are four head-men sitting in the sun dance lodge around a drum, and every now and then they sing and beat the drum.

Now my dance is started. I have prayed to the Manitou for rain. The good Manitou is in the sun, and the bad Manitou is in the ground. Everything is going all right. Always these sun dances were held about the tenth of June. That was about the time when, if it were a dry year, rain was expected.

Now, the Chief medicine man who is next in power to the Chief comes into the tent with a bundle of clothes, a horse, or anything the Indian who wants to become a medicine man has given him. The Indian comes in crying to the Manitou, "Have mercy on me! Have mercy on me!"

The medicine man puts down his presents, and goes to the Indian. He examines him all over. If he thinks he is not fit to be a brave, or a medicine man, he advises him that he will not be able to stand the hardship. If he considers him fit, he makes him sit down. Then he opens his medicine bag and takes out all his medicines, roots, leaves, twigs, berries, all tied in little rags.

The Indian takes off his shirt. The medicine man takes a sharp pocket-knife, lifts the skin of the man's breast, doubles it, and makes a slit right through the double fold. He does the same thing to the other side of the breast, then he takes his shaggannappi (made especially for this purpose), which has been well vermilioned, and runs it through the slits. If the Indian can stand these incisions without fainting, he has got the making of a brave.

Now, the medicine man takes the end of the long lines of shaggannappi and ties them to the centre tree. He ties them so that they run in a slanting position to the man's body. This done, he gives the Indian a shove backward from the tree, and tells him to go and dance, to bend his body backward and to dance on the backs of his heels. The Indian, unless he faints, in which case water is poured on him until he comes to, dances once to the right and twice to the left, and has got to keep this up from sunrise to sunset.

All day the Indian is required to dance, leaning backward to the slant of the shaggannappi. If he can stand it all day, he is declared a brave. Sometimes the skin on the breast would stretch six inches. The medicine man would put medicine on the wound to prevent it from bleeding.

This is the way the sun dance went on—always for four days. I saw sun dances in the sixties when the Indians had the strong buffalo meat. Then the Indians could make braves. They could dance all day. When, later, the Indians got other food, they could not make braves. The young Indians could not dance more than half a day.

The North-West was overrun with boodlers in the sixties and seventies. Some called them whiskey traders; now they would be called bootleggers. They got their liquor from St. Paul, Minnesota. They were rivals of the regular traders, and of the Hudson's Bay Company.

There was one big boodler named William Dace who had a store at Pembina Mountain. Once when his brigade of two hundred carts loaded with liquor and driven by thirty or forty men was on its way from Saint Paul, he found that two of his men were drunk most of the time.

He could not imagine where his men were getting the alcohol—none of the casks had been broached. He could not understand it. Well, it was like this. One day one of these drivers was lying on his back under one of the carts, resting. Idly, he bored a hole with his gimlet up through the floor of the cart. It penetrated the cask, and when he withdrew the gimlet, the liquor began to flow. He had a good drink; then he made a peg and placed it in the gimlet hole.

He took his friend into his confidence. Whenever either one wanted a drink, he crawled under the cart, and withdrew the peg. It was not until Dace's cargo was unloaded and the empty cask discovered that the secret was disclosed.

That reminds me of the time I "fooled" Inspector Herchmer[2] of the Mounted Police. It was on one of my trips to Fort Garry for supplies. My permit for twenty-four two-gallon kegs of Hudson's Bay rum had not arrived. The Hudson's Bay agent said, "Welsh, if you want to take a chance, I will give you the rum." Time was important to me. My Red River carts were packed, my ponies rested. The Indians would be waiting for supplies, ready with their finest buffalo robes. I decided to take a chance. It was a big one, too, because the penalty for taking rum into the Territories without a permit was severe.

I bought the rum, and early next morning packed it on my carts. We travelled as far as Shoal Lake where we camped that night. The next morning Herchmer of the Mounted Police rode up. He rode around the carts and called, "Whose camp is this?"

"This is Welsh's camp," I replied.

"What have you got on board?"

"I have got everything on board."

I told him to look around. Then I opened a big bottle of brandy that I kept for this kind of thing, filled a big tumbler, and gave it to him. He drank the brandy and galloped away. This is how the old liquor permits read:

2. Herchmer—At one time Commission of the Royal North-West Mounted Police, Regina, Saskatchewan, Canada.

Liquor Permit   North-West Territories.
Not transferable.   Battleford.

                                        . . . . June, 18. . .

                                        Mr. . . . .
No. . . . . . .
Of Qu'Appelle . . . . is permitted to take into the
North-West Territories . . . . Gallons Brandy . . . . .for
medicinal purposes.

                                        David Laird.

Certified.
    A.E. Forget.

Herchmer was a fine fellow. In after years we laughed
about this little joke. You see he had let me through on my
reputation. It pays to have a good reputation.

CHAPTER NINETEEN

A Judge for a Passenger

I remember another trip, one that I made with Judge Ryan.[1] He was a member of the first Council of the North-West Territories that met at Livingstone, Swan River District, on March 7th, 1877. Everybody in the North-West knew Judge Ryan.

In November of 1876, he was on his way from Battleford to Fort Garry. He asked me if I would drive him from Fort Qu'Appelle to Shoal Lake, Manitoba, going by way of Fort Pelly. He had come from Battleford by waggon. Fort Pelly is one hundred and twenty-five miles north-east of Fort Qu'Appelle. I said, "Look here, Mr. Ryan, before we do anything I want to know how much you will pay me to take you to Shoal Lake."

He asked me how seven dollars and fifty cents a day would be. It wasn't a very good price, I told him, because it was getting late in the season, and we would likely have a very cold trip. He said that he had been paying that price right along. I asked him who would provide the grub. He replied that he would find the grub himself, and pay for everything that I wanted until I got back home. All that I would have to provide would be the light democrat, the horses, the tent, and of course my time. I agreed to his terms.

I asked him when he would be ready to start. The next

1. Judge Ryan was on his way to Fort Livingstone to swear Lieutenant-Governor Laird and his Council into office on November 27th, 1876. Fort Livingstone was the first capital of the North-West Territories, 1876–1877.

morning, he said. That would be Tuesday. I got him on board at the Mission at Lebret the next morning, and we started for Fort Pelly. We drove all day, and made good time.

We camped that night beyond and north of Pheasant Forks. It was very cloudy. It looked like snow. We camped under the poplar trees. When I got up the next morning my horses were gone. I had a boy with me, so I told him to cook the breakfast; that I would go after the horses.

I threw my saddle over my shoulder and started off on the run. About three-quarters of a mile from camp I found the horses. As I was getting on horseback, I heard a gun shot from the camp. By God, I thought, I hope they haven't shot each other. Then I heard some one yelling.

It seems that this old fellow, the judge, was an amateur boxer, because as soon as I had gone he began to spar and pretend to box with the boy. As the old man was having fun, two prairie chickens came and lit on the trees under the tent. The boy, seeing the chickens, ran for the gun to shoot them.

The judge, not seeing the chickens, seized the boy and began to shout, "For God's sake don't shoot." But the boy fired and killed the chickens. When the judge saw the chickens fall he was all right. When he saw me coming, he came and told me all about the affair; that they had been having a little fun, and that the joke was on him.

We had breakfast. Then we hitched up and made for Fort Pelly. When we got there, we stayed with McBeath, the Factor at the Hudson's Bay Post.

The judge asked if we had everything in the way of grub for the remainder of the trip. I told him I thought we had enough to last us to where we were going, the Swan River Barracks. Long ago there was a regular little town there and a detachment of Mounted Police. It was at this point the Government was planning to build a railroad.

We got to the Barracks. The judge had a good big house of his own with about ten rooms in it. We took our baggage there. Ryan told me that we would stop at Swan River for a day. He had business there with the officer in charge of the

Mounted Police. I told him it made no difference to me how long we stopped, as long as my pay went on.

Now I had a bad pain in my back. Ryan said he would take me to see a military doctor who was stationed there, and who would fix me up for life. We went. The doctor told me I had strained my back. At that time, I was calculated to be a very strong man for my size. I could put a thousand pounds on a Red River cart, then get under it, and lift it with my back. That's how I had strained my back.

The doctor made me up a bottle of medicine, and told me to guard it as I would my eyes, not to let it freeze, and not to take it until I got home to Lebret. He told me to take a spoonful of medicine three times a day, and to tie a yard (doubled) of red flannel sprinkled with sulphur around my bare hide. He warned me not to get my feet cold.

We went around and examined the town. You couldn't imagine the amount of stuff that was lying around there. Telegraph wires, telegraph poles, everything for building a railroad. The judge told me that I wouldn't believe how much money had been spent on stuff that we saw lying in piles—rotting.

When the Liberals were in power they had started to build a railroad (the Canadian Pacific) from Winnipeg to Edmonton, and through that north country to Vancouver. They planned to build it in ten years.

Then Sir John A. MacDonald got into power. He was a Conservative. His Government decided instead to run the railroad where it is to-day. Sir John wanted the road run from ocean to ocean as quickly as possible. All that stuff that was at Swan River has rotted there. We saw no buffalo as we travelled—only deer.

The next day we started for Shoal Lake. I thought we would follow, as we had been doing, the old Hudson's Bay trail, but the judge wanted me to take him right across country, hills and everything. He said he wanted to see that country. I told him that the trip would be hard on my horses and on me because we would have to go over hills and through bush where I had never been before, that we might go astray.

"Oh, you are an old traveller. I have never heard of an old traveller losing his way," he said.

You see Judge Ryan hadn't been long enough in the country to know how easily travellers could get lost in this great North-West. Well, I told him that we would go back on the trail about three miles, and get directions from a man, an Indian I knew.

We got to Chief Kow-e-zanse's place. He was the Chief of the Fort Pelly Indian Reserve. I asked him to give me the direction. He told me there was a trail across country, and that if I watched carefully I would be able to pick it up here and there. He showed me where this trail began. We got on very well.

Before noon the next day, we got to the Indian Reserve at Lizard Point. There were Cree and Chipewyan Indians in this reserve. It was early, but I advised the judge to stop here for dinner, so that we would have a long afternoon on the trail. That would suit him, he said.

We went into the Chief's house. His name was Oo-ma-ka-kee (the frog). He had a comfortable house, and two wives who looked very clean. I told the Chief that we would have our lunch at his house. He asked me how we would like some deer meat. He had killed a deer the day before.

The offer was all right for me, but I did not know whether the judge would accept it. I translated our conversation for the judge. He would be pleased to accept it, he said. Then he asked me if I would get the women to warm some water for him to wash. I had been washing in the snow—there was snow on the ground now—but the judge was a tenderfoot. He wouldn't do that.

The Indian wives prepared a fine meal. They cooked deer meat, French fried potatoes, and made fine bannock, and tea. The judge enjoyed it. When we were going, the judge offered the Chief two dollars, but he would not accept it. It was not for him, the judge told him, but for his wives. The Frog took the money.

We left Lizzard's Point and made for Birtle, Manitoba, a distance of fifteen miles. When we got there we camped in an Indian house to save time putting up our tent. This house was very clean, too. Next day we made Shoal Lake. The judge asked me how long it would take me to get home by following the trail. I told him four days. He paid me for seven days. He said that I had been good to him and we parted. The judge went from there by stage to Fort Garry. I started for Lebret, which I reached in four days.

CHAPTER TWENTY

I Go Ranching

It was in the fall of 1884 that I decided to give up farming and go back to Round Plain and take up a ranch. My wife told me she thought I was going to make a bad move, but I told her there was nothing like trying. She understood that when I said a thing I meant it.

I got ready and started for Round Plain. When I got there I found a few of my neighbors still there—half-breeds that I had known when I wintered at this place. One was Charles Trottier. They were surprised to see me, and glad, too. They asked me what I was going to do. I told them it was my intention to take up a claim of land—to start a settlement. Now, I told them, we would have to plow in the ground to make a living, because there were no longer any buffalo.

"Hurrah!" they cried and clapped their hands.

I stayed with my friends that night. The next morning I started out to select my own land—my claim. I had wintered and done business there for so many years that I knew every bit of the country, and the best spot to select.

I picked my land on the north end of Round Plain. Of course, this land was not surveyed. This Round Plain was eleven miles long and three miles broad. It was on the bank of the south branch of the Saskatchewan River. I took up a whole section of land; a half-section for myself, and a half-section for my boys.

The position of my claim lay just one mile back from the river bank and extended to a big slough. I knew I would be able to cut hundreds of tons of hay every year in this slough. This would, I felt sure, make an excellent ranching location.

It was now the beginning of September. I had brought my plow and harness, so I broke three acres of land that could be used for a potato and vegetable garden in the spring. The plowing marked my claim. Nobody else would take it. That was the law of the country.

I had brought my mower with me, too, so now I hitched up my horses and cut hay in the slough. I mowed for two and a half days, cut a strip one mile long. We raked, hauled, and stacked the hay. We had one hundred loads. When I finished the hay, I built a little shack sixteen feet square. By this time it was November. I asked my brother-in-law, who was living there, if he would mud my shack while I went back to Lebret to fetch my stock—I had a lot of stock—before it got too cold. He agreed.

I found my friends at Round Plain all excited. Trottier asked me if Dumont had been speaking to me about Riel. When I said that he had not, Trottier said I had better hear what he had to say.

When I saw Dumont he told me that he was going to bring Riel back from across the line. Riel had fled to the States after the Red River Rebellion.

I said to Dumont, "Let me cross-question you a little. What is your intention? Riel is well off in the States. He is better there. If I understand you right, you are going to get this man into trouble."

He asked me, in a very independent way, why I thought so, and said that whatever plans the other half-breeds made— of course I always called myself a half-breed although I had only a little Indian blood—I always thought that I understood things better than the others.

"I think I understand this business better than any of you here," I said, "for I have been in this kind of situation before, and you haven't." I meant that I had seen the result of the Red River uprising for I was going back and forth from the plains to Fort Garry at the time. Then I asked him what he wanted, and if he were dissatisfied with something. He replied that some of the other half-breeds were dissatisfied; that they wanted their rights and their scrip, and that they had engaged Riel to help them.

"Your rights and scrip? You say you want your scrip, Dumont? I saw you draw your scrip in Winnipeg. You drew one hundred and sixty acres for yourself, and one hundred and sixty acres for your wife. All your friends who were there got the same as you. I saw that with my own eyes," I told him.

He said that was true, but that the other people in the North-West wanted to get scrip, too. I asked him why he hadn't explained that he wanted to get scrip for these people in the North-West and not for himself. He said he had not thought of that. I advised him to let these people alone, to let them be quiet. I had got my scrip and was satisfied. He had got his and should be satisfied.

"Welsh, we can never do anything to suit you," he replied. "If anything happened that didn't suit you, you would turn around and shoot your own children."

"Look here, Dumont," I said. "We need not go any further. I have no time to speak to you to-day. I am a working man and you are a loafer. You have all the time you want. I will not listen to you. If I understand you, Dumont, you want to bring Riel here to start a rebellion. Speak up like a man. Speak the truth. Isn't that what you want to do? Answer me."

He replied that it was so, and I asked him, "Where are you going to get your men, your money, your supplies, your ammunition? Now, to cut the thing short, I am not going to talk to you. I have a big day's work ahead of me. If you raise a rebellion, nothing will come of it. You will have to leave the country and leave your people here."

It was December now. Three days after Dumont had come to see me, I started for Lebret. We had five jumpers loaded with furs—rats, mink, beaver, otter, wolf, badger, and bear, but no buffalo robes. I had a boy from the settlement to help me.

We started at noon from the river. We camped that night where the town of Dundurn now stands. It was prairie then with a little scattered bush. It was forty below when we got up in the morning. The boy, young Trottier, thought we had better turn back; that we were in for a spell of bad weather. I told him that that was something I had never done in my life, turn back on the road, no matter how stormy or cold the weather. I offered to let him go back if he wanted to, but he said he would stay with me. That was the kind of man I liked to meet, I answered.

This was the tenth of December, and I wanted to get home for Christmas. From Dundurn there was a space of twenty miles before we would strike the bush again. It was so stormy that we were not sure whether we could keep our direction. We covered the twenty miles and hit the bush late in the evening. This bush was called the Indian side woods.

We gathered a lot of wood, put up our tent, set up our camp stove, and hobbled our horses. It had been a bad day, travelling all day in a raging blizzard. We both felt tired. I had never felt so tired in all my travels as I felt that day.

The next morning we started off again. It was not quite so stormy, but, by heavens, it was cold! I had felt tired in the morning which was unusual for me. We made for the west end of Long Lake for our second encampment—for dinner. That was a distance of twenty-five miles. After dinner we started again. We cut across the lake in a north-easterly direction. In all we travelled about forty miles that day.

We camped where there was wood and water. My legs felt stiff, but I thought it was the cold weather and running in the snow that caused the stiffness. We had no snowshoes, and anyway we couldn't drive a band of jumpers and keep up to them on snowshoes. We had to walk and run all day beside our jumpers. If we had ridden in the jumpers, we would have frozen. It was not the strength a man had in those days, it was the pluck that was in him. The next morning we started again.

About ten o'clock that night we reached Piapot's Reserve. We got to the farm Instructor's home. McKinnon was surprised to see me. He said he thought I was at Dundurn.

I explained that I was on my way to Lebret, and asked him if we could have dinner, and some feed for our horses.

"Everything that you want, Welsh," he said.

We had a very good dinner. Beef, pork, potatoes, and everything fine. When I told McKinnon that my legs were stiff, he asked me to stay at his place for the night; I could easily get home, only thirty miles, the next day. I thought, this is a good offer, why be stupid, better accept. I did.

Next morning we started off very early. We had travelled half the distance, about fifteen miles, when my legs got so stiff that I could hardly walk.

We decided to stop at the house of Baptiste Robilliard, who was pretty well off. He had lots to eat and drink, and had lots of hay. We stayed there that night. We played pedro until twelve o'clock.

Next morning my legs were so painful that I could scarcely walk. It was terribly cold, and I had to ride most of the way. We got home about noon. I told my wife that my legs were sore, that we had had a very rough trip, and asked her to give me a good dose of brandy and to let me sleep until supper-time.

I suspected that I had caught gout from Bannatyne who, when we travelled together, had made me sleep with him. The intense cold had aggravated it.

The next day I felt worse. My legs were all swollen and black. I asked my wife to have my man hitch the horse to the cutter and put the robes in, and told her that I would drive to the Fort to see the doctor. I drove to the hotel. I had a great friend at the Fort. His name was William Clarke. He saw me drive up and get out of the cutter. "What's the matter, Welsh?" he asked. I told him that I had caught gout from Bannatyne and had come to see the doctor.

Clarke asked me to go along to the stables with him—to let him see my legs. I did. He said, "Yes, that's gout. Oh, hell! the doctor is no good for your gout. Have you got twenty-five cents?"

I gave him twenty-five cents, then he said, "Go into the

hotel bar-room and ask Bob Smith, the bar-keeper, to give you a good hot drink." I did. Soon Clarke came in with a little bottle about the size of the end of my thumb. He asked me to go upstairs to a room with him and he would tell me a secret.

"Welsh," he said, "if you had gone to the doctor you would have spent hundreds of dollars on your gout, and he wouldn't have helped you. You are a good friend to me, and a good friend to my sons, and I'll cure your gout if you will do what I tell you. This remedy will either kill or cure you."

Then he told me the secret of the medicine. He told me to go home, take a piece of loaf sugar, sprinkle fifteen drops of this medicine on the sugar, and swallow it. I was to repeat the dose the next day. He also warned me that if I took more or less than fifteen drops I would be a dead man.

When I told my wife this, she was horrified. I asked her not to be afraid, that I was well prepared, and that if I had to die, I would die. She held the sugar. I counted the drops. She counted the drops. I said "fifteen." She said "fourteen." "Fifteen!" I said, and ate the sugar.

I slept as solidly as a rock. They tried to waken me during the night, but couldn't. Next morning, at five, I awoke. My wife was glad to find me alive. The swelling that had been up to my waist had gone down to my knees. That night I took another dose of the medicine.[1] The next morning all swelling had disappeared. I was all right. I have never had gout since.

Clarke was a farmer, but he had at one time studied medicine. He died several years ago. I have never told anybody the secret of the cure for gout. It is good to be friendly with everybody.

---

1. Probably urine—an Indian remedy for gout.

Chapter Twenty-one

I Fall Foul of Louis Riel

9 spent just twenty-five days at Lebret. At the end of that time I began thinking about my people at Round Plain who expected me back with supplies. I had come for supplies to start my own trading-post on the Saskatchewan River, as well as to get my stock.

I started back with nine jumpers well loaded with goods. I had forty sacks of flour and bacon, sugar, tea, tobacco, lard—all the things that were necessary. There were quite a few families settled at Round Plain. My livestock followed the jumpers.

The trip was hard. There was no trail. When I got to Touchwood, I met Père Lebret. He had been out on a Mission. He was glad to see me and appeared to be very jolly. I asked him, "Father, what makes you so jolly?"

"Welsh," he answered, "I haven't had anything to eat for two days. I want you to give me something."

Provisions were very scarce at Touchwood. He asked me if I had any bread. I told him that I had bannock, salt pork, beef, everything; that I would stop right there and cook him a meal. He replied that he was in a hurry. He was driving. "Just give me a little and I will go on," he said.

I gave him two bannocks, a little can of lard, a piece of pork, some tea and sugar. Poor Father Lebret! The Fathers were all good, but he was something special—extra good.

We stopped that night at Touchwood. We had horses hauling heavy loads that were not as good as they should have been. I had hired some freighters, too, and their horses were very poor—useless. I said to my men, "I must stop here to-day. I must trade, make some bargains. Things don't suit me."

I had all day to do business. I went around and saw the settlers. I exchanged two of my poor horses for one good one. I got another good one for one of mine and a little extra in trade. When I got through trading, we had seven good fat horses.

The freighters had made a good trail from Touchwood to Fish Creek. This was a roundabout way to reach Round Plain—'twas a good day's travel longer than going across country—but I decided to go this way in order to save the horses. We put in hard days.

When we got to Fish Creek this freighter of mine—he had eighteen sacks of flour—said he couldn't go any farther. I asked him why, since his horses were keeping up with the rest and he didn't have to lead. He told me he would take the flour on to Round Plain, but that I would have to pay him a little more. I told him that he had agreed to deliver the eighteen sacks of flour at my wintering ground for a certain price, and that I would pay him no more. He wasn't willing to do this.

I asked him to bring his jumper alongside of mine. I unloaded the flour off it, putting two sacks on each of my five jumpers. Then I told this freighter, Baptiste Roi, that I would take off so much for freighting the flour from Fish Creek to Round Plain. I paid him and told him to go.

It would take me three more days to get home. I had eight sacks of flour that I couldn't carry, so I decided to leave them with a man by the name of Hooey whom I knew very well. I would have to come back to Batoche in a month for my mail, and could come to Fish Creek then for the flour.

I got to Round Plain. We were just twelve days coming from Lebret. The people were getting out of grub. I supplied them with provisions again. And so the thing carried on that way, and there wasn't a word spoken about Gabriel Dumont or Riel. I thought to myself that everything must be knocked in the head.

About a month later, I decided to go to Batoche to get my mail. Batoche was sixty miles from Round Plain. I asked my brother-in-law, Frank Boyer, if he would round up the cattle and horses, see if they were all right, and watch them while I was away. I would go on to Batoche from Fish Creek—sixteen miles north of Batoche along the Saskatchewan River—to get the mail, then back to Fish Creek to pick up my flour.

On the sixteenth day of March, 1885, I reached Saskatoon in time for dinner. I met Dr. Willoughby. He asked me if I were going to turn back from here. I told him I was on my way to Batoche to get my mail, and would then go back to Fish Creek to pick up some flour I had left there the month before.

Willoughby had a man keeping a store for him at Fish Creek, and he wanted to go to Fish Creek to see this man, so he asked if I would take him. I told him I would take him to Fish Creek, but that I couldn't bring him back because I would have a heavy load—flour, baggage, and provisions. He said he would go with me after dinner.

We had a fine dinner at his house. As we were travelling along after dinner, I looked at Willoughby. His face looked all green. I was sitting in the front part of the jumper, Willoughby was sitting in the back, but we were facing each other. I said, "Look here, Doctor, are you sick? You are losing your color. You look green."

He replied that he was just going to say the same to me. I looked up at the sky. It was almost dark. There was an eclipse of the sun. This was on the 16th of March, 1885.

At Clark's crossing we picked up another man named McIntyre who wanted to go to Fish Creek. About three miles before we got to Willoughby's store at Fish Creek, we stopped at Baptiste Rochelle's place for dinner. Then we went on to the Doctor's store to camp for the night after getting our mail.

While we were in the store, Norbert DeLorme came in. He told me that I had struck a bad time. I asked him what he meant. He said that it was reported that Willoughby, McIntyre and I were out scouting for the Government. I told him that there must be a liar around somewhere.

Then he said that Dumont had gone to One Arrow's Reserve to collect the Indians to raise trouble. He advised me to see Gabriel before we went to his place, which was between Fish Creek and Batoche—nearer Fish Cree. Then DeLorme[1] left.

We had been talking in French. Willoughby asked me what DeLorme and I had been talking about. I told him that it looked as if we were going to get into trouble, that Gabriel Dumont and Riel were holding a big meeting in the church at Batoche that night, and that in the morning they were going to start a rebellion. At least, that was what DeLorme had told me. And, I added, it looked suspicious, for when we had gone to Batoche for our mail, we had seen a big crowd of people gathered.

Willoughby wanted me to hitch my mare to the jumper and start for home right away. I told him to go on his own legs if he wanted to, that I was not the kind of man to run away from other men.

Willoughby and McIntyre sat talking about having had dinner at Rochelle's house. I was tired, so I laid down and slept. I awoke at twelve o'clock. I thought, Dumont will be back from the meeting at Batoche now. I got up and went over to DeLorme's house. Dumont hadn't arrived yet. I told DeLorme that Dumont must have gone through, but he said that Dumont would be sure to stop and see him. I said I would wait. I did. But I was tired and sleepy and, as DeLorme didn't offer me a bed, I walked back after a while to Willoughby's store.

1. Delorme—An important family in early Canadian history. Henry's Journal; Elliott Coues editor, page 193: Delorme or De Lorme was a common name; the one meant in the text is no further specified.—Pierre De Lorme was one of the men who started on Sir Alexander McKenzie's memorable voyage to the Arctic Ocean, June 3rd, 1879,—François Delorme is listed as of N.W. Co., Lower Red R., 1799.—One Delorme of the N.W. Co. was with Thompson at the fort near the forks of the Peace R., summer and fall of 1803 . . . "Mr." Delorme of N.W. Co. was sent by Henry to summer at Portage la Prairie, 1804 . . . One Delorme was a freeman at Winnipeg, Aug. 10, 1898.—François Enos, dit Delorme, was a witness in the Semple case at Toronto, Oct. 18, 1818.

Willoughby and McIntyre were both waiting for me. I went to bed. Just as I was falling asleep, I heard a scratch at the door. It sounded like a dog scratching. I thought this was DeLorme, who was sly and sneaky and would not knock like a man. I did not answer. I learned later that it was Dumont. He had wanted to speak to me, but was suspicious of the other men.

DeLorme had told me that Riel was staying with Gabriel Azure and his wife, and that if I wanted to speak to him I would find him there. The next morning I decided to see Riel and find out what he was going to do. I went to the door of Gabriel Azure's house. Azure's wife answered my knock. She said that Riel was not there, but that I would find him at Baptiste Rochelle's.

I told McIntyre and Willoughby that we would go to Rochelle's again, have dinner and see Riel and Dumont. We started. There was a thick bluff in front of Rochelle's house. This house had a lot of big windows. As we drew near we could see through these windows, a lot of people sitting around. Gabriel saw us coming, jumped up, and came out.

I gave my horse a lash, made her step out, and almost shoved her head into the house through the open door. The men who came out asked me where I was going. To have dinner with them, I said. I jumped out of the sleigh. Gabriel told a boy to unhitch my horse and put him in the stable.

I told Gabriel that this was very good of him. I took my grub sack, and Willoughby took his. We went into the house and threw our grub sacks on the floor. I said, "There is quite a crowd here, but I think there is enough in those sacks for all."

Rochelle said that that was very good. He ordered his wife and daughter to get a meal. They set two big tables. We could sit down, fifty people at a time.

When I entered the house, I recognized Riel at once from his photograph. He began to walk back and forth in the house. Remember, they thought we were Government spies. Finally Riel went up to Willoughby, asked him his name, and what church he belonged to. Willoughby was terribly scared. He turned pale and answered that he was a Presbyterian.

Riel said, "That is the root of the devil."

Riel then went to McIntyre and asked him the same questions. He got the same reply about religion. Riel said, "You are a good-hearted man, and a charitable man."

Now he came to me.

"Welsh," he said, "I want you to give me your name in full." I asked, "In full?" He said, "Yes."

I had just got a couple of letters from my wife and children. I pulled them out of my pocket, showed them to him and said, "There's my address in full."

He looked at the letters and said, "Welsh, they tell me that you are not a true half-breed."

"Whoever told you that," I said, "bring him before me, and I will settle with them." I meant Dumont and Trottier. They were displeased with me for not joining them.

Riel said, "Welsh, I'll give you just one week to pray and make up with your God."

"A whole week to live," I replied. "That's a lot of time."

Riel stopped speaking to me and called Dumont over to the corner of the room where they spoke together in low voices. But I'm like a cat. I hear a lot.

Riel said to Dumont, "You can let Welsh and his men go through. They are not spies, as you suspected. Let them go through. We'll get them later."

Chapter Twenty-two

In the Throes of a Rebellion

We did not have dinner after all. The people got offended. Riel was the most important man there. He was the leader, you might say. He was the first man seated. The table filled up. About fifty men sat in. Riel blessed the table; then he jumped up and said that he was not going to have any dinner.

When we heard him say that, we all got up and left the food. I thought Riel was fine looking, but I thought also that he had more education than brains.

I asked Gabriel Dumont if he would have my horse hitched. I said that I wanted to reach Clark's Crossing that night. He did.

Riel said to Dumont, "I will take half the crowd with me, and half the crowd will stay with you. I'll go and take Walter's and Baker's store." This was a big store there. They left immediately. I counted the men again. Forty-five went and forty-five were left.

McIntyre, Willoughby and I got into the jumper and drove sixteen miles before stopping for dinner. It was about four o'clock now. Willoughby wanted to push on to Saskatoon, sixteen miles farther, that night. I told him I would drive no farther that day, but would spend the night where we were and get an early start in the morning.

When we reached Saskatoon, at ten o'clock next day, all was excitement. News had come through by wire that Riel and his followers had taken up arms. Women and children were crying. Sleighs were loaded with people ready to flee to Moose Jaw.

When the people saw me coming, men, women and children began calling, "Here's Welsh! Here's Welsh! He will fix us up. He will tell us what to do."

Trounce, the mayor, or headman,[1] came and asked me if it would be advisable to call a meeting. They all wanted me to tell them what I knew and thought about this trouble, this rebellion. I asked him to call a meeting for two o'clock, and said that I would spend the night in Saskatoon. He spread the news that I would address a meeting at two o'clock.

At two o'clock I could hardly make my way through the crowds to the town hall! Everybody was terrified and kept calling, "Mr. Welsh, Mr. Welsh." I stepped to the platform and addressed them.

"Ladies and gentlemen," I began, "I am sorry to see such a disturbance and everybody so frightened. But there is no sense in you getting into your sleighs and travelling to Moose Jaw. You would be four or five days on the road. There are no houses on the way. You would have to drag wood for fires. It would mean great hardship for the women and children. There would be more people frozen to death than if they stayed here and took a chance of being shot. The Indians and half-breeds are not dogs. They will not come and shoot you down without notifying you. If there is a man in a bad fix, I am that man. Dr. Willoughby will tell you that Riel has given me one week to live. And do you think I fear Riel's threat?"

Willoughby came forward and confirmed what I had said about Riel, but he did not tell them that I had practically saved his life.

Trounce then got up and addressed the meeting. He told the people that they had better listen to my advice which, he said, was good. He advised them to go home, put their horses in the stables and remain quiet. So they did.

The next morning I hitched up and went on to Round

1. William Henry Trounce: Saskatoon 1883 to 1886; a leader in the community.

156

Plain. I found everything all right. I didn't tell the people in the settlement anything about the trouble at Fish Creek. I wanted to find out what they knew. I was not in their confidence. They knew I disapproved of Dumont's attitude.

Time went on and nothing was said. On the third night after I got home, I heard a big noise around my house. I got up and looked out. There were about forty men on horseback surrounding my house. I opened the door and two men, Baptiste Carrière and François Vermette, tried to enter, but I closed and locked the door.

The half-breeds spoke through the door and asked me the amount of supplies I had on hand. I told them it was none of their business. They told me that I would hand things out when White Cap came along, for he was in the group. I told them that White Cap was my best friend and to bring him along.

White Cap had some of his band with him, but most of the crowd were half-breeds. I told White Cap that I would give no supplies to the half-breeds, and if they wanted to fight I was ready. White Cap replied that I had always been a strong man, that I had a strong heart (chanda soota). Then he told the crowd to go home, to come again in the morning, and to treat me in a decent way. He said they should ask for things, not demand them. So they did.

I was aware that the rebellion was really in progress, so that night, fearing that my stores would be seized, I got my brother-in-law, who was working for me, but who knew nothing of Riel's movements, to help me hide all my ammunition, some flour, and other supplies.

Next morning the same crowd came back. White Cap asked me if I were going to give them my goods. I asked him if he had an order from anyone to get supplies. Vermette and Carrière said that Gabriel Dumont and Maxime Lepine had given them very definite orders to seize my stores, and, in addition to that, they were to take me prisoner.

"Ho! Ho! Vermette, you haven't got me yet," I laughed.

They had to have food for the troops, they said. They seized everything I had—foodstuffs, cattle and horses. I asked

Vermette who would pay me for this stuff. He said they had been told to tell me that if the half-breeds won they would pay; if they lost the Government would pay. I couldn't do anything. I was only one man against that crowd. I could easily have shot a dozen or so of these men before they had time to move, but what was the use?

Vermette and Carrière decided, after sending the others on with my stuff, to take me prisoner. They wanted me to hitch up and go with them immediately. I told them that they could wait my convenience; that I would not go until the next morning. These men were a little afraid of me. I could have shot them both, but I didn't. They were under Dumont's orders. I thought I would go with them, and see what was happening.

We started next morning and overtook the brigade about a mile south of Saskatoon. Soon a rider came galloping up. He wanted to know where Welsh was. My guards pointed out my tent. He rapped at my tent door, and told me that Mayor Trounce, of Saskatoon, wanted me right away. He carried a letter from the Mayor. I told him I was a prisoner, but would speak to the two headmen of the brigade, Trottier and White Cap.

I went to Trottier and told him that the Mayor of Saskatoon wanted me right away. I showed him the letter. He said that I would have to see White Cap. I went to White Cap. He said he would agree to let me go if Trottier would. We went back to Trottier's tent. He said that I could go on one condition, that I let two of his men go with me to hear what Trounce had to say.

We mounted our horses and galloped to the town hall in Saskatoon. My guards were invited to sit in the second seat from the platform. Trounce drew me aside to talk. I told my guards that I would be right back. Trounce asked me if I knew how the rebellion was going. I told him I had not heard any details.

He told me that a policeman had been shot dead at Duck Lake; that Captain Moore of Prince Albert had got two legs broken; that two Indians had been killed, and that Gabriel Dumont's brother and his cousin had been shot dead. I told him they must be having a rebellion in earnest. He replied that things looked bad, and that he had sent for me to talk things over.

He asked me to step into another room with him. My guards did not follow. He showed me stacks of repeating rifles and a great supply of ammunition. Then he told me that the townspeople had got strict orders from the Government not to let White Cap's brigade go through, because some of White Cap's Indians had complained that they were being forced into the rebellion by the half-breeds. There were about forty men in White Cap's brigade, and twenty in Trottier's. Not more than sixty men altogether.

Also there were two bosses to this brigade. White Cap was boss of the Indians. Trottier was boss of the half-breeds. Trounce asked me if I could help him find out whether the Sioux were being forced into a rebellion, without getting myself into further trouble.

"Mr. Trounce," I said, "if you will go with me we will soon find out. But not to-night. We all want a good sleep. We will see about it in the morning. You understand, there are two brigades, White Cap's and Trottier's. They will have to go right through the town of Saskatoon. You will take one side of the road. I will take the other. When they enter the town, we will call a halt. Then we will ask each man who goes through if he is being forced into the rebellion."

"You are a great man. I knew you would be able to advise and help. That is why I sent for you," Trounce said.

I asked Trounce which side of the road he would take. He answered that he could not speak Sioux, but only English, and a little French. I told him he could be a half-breed next day. I would be a Sioux. Then I asked him if anybody in the town could speak Sioux, and said that if there were he could be secured to interpret my conversation with White Cap.

He answered, "No, but I have faith in what you say, Welsh. I trust you."

That decided the thing. We returned to the hall. I called to my guards, and we returned to camp. Trottier and White Cap were waiting for me. I told them what Trounce had said—that orders had come from the Government to stop White Cap and his Indians, who were claiming that the half-breeds were forcing them to join Riel.

White Cap declared that the rumor was not true, and that he and his band would go through, that nobody would stop him. Then I said, "White Cap, to-morrow I will walk with you fellows to the town. White Cap, you will be on my side of the road. If you give each man of your brigade permission to go through of his own free will I will let him go through. It will be the same with Trottier's brigade. Trounce will question them."

I asked Trottier which side of the road he would take. He said the right. I told him that I would take the left.

Morning came. It was time to start. The flag was hoisted.[2] That was a sign to go. Trottier started. Then White Cap followed. I had put in my rig, which was the last one of all, some provisions to use on the trail. I had a bull dog revolver in my belt.

We got to Saskatoon. Everything went off as we had arranged. Trounce and Trottier took one side of the road, and White Cap and I the other. Each man was challenged as he went through, and asked if he were going to join Riel of his own will. When the last rig went through, I jumped into my rig, wheeled my horse around, and said, "I'm the only man that's forced to go through, and I won't go through. Good-bye," I called to the warriors. They were surprised but went on. That is how Trounce and I saved Saskatoon.

I stayed with a man by the name of Wright, a farmer. Trottier and White Cap camped two miles beyond Saskatoon. They were on their way to Clark's Crossing. At the end of that day my brother-in-law, Frank Boyer, who had gone with them, came after me. He said that Trottier wanted very

---

2. Always when the fur brigades travelled over the prairie, the hoisting of a flag—usually a Hudson's Bay Company flag—was the signal to start or stop.

much to see me. I told him to return and tell Charles Trottier, my uncle, that I would have nothing to do with him, that if he had anything to say, he could come to me. That was my answer.

I stayed with Wright for five days. He was very kind and did not want to take pay for my board, but I gave him a sack of flour, ninety-eight pounds, which was worth ten dollars. Flour was very scarce then.

A man by the name of Smudge, of Saskatoon, heard that I was going to Lebret. He came to me and said, "My God, will you take me with you?" I thought I would be five days on the road without company. I decided to take the poor devil. We started, and reached Lebret on the afternoon of the fifth day.

White Cap was a great warrior. He belonged to Sitting Bull's band that fled to Canada from the United States after the Custer Massacre. All White Cap's band were great warriors. Years ago, before I began to trade, the Sioux used to attack the half-breed hunters, so the Indians and half-breeds got together and agreed to sign a treaty.

This treaty, between the Sioux and half-breed buffalo hunters, was signed on the plains south-west of Pembina Mountain, on English territory. Batiste La Bombarbe was the interpreter. He told me about it. A great many Sioux Indians, including nine chiefs, met with a big band of buffalo hunters and signed a treaty not to fight or attack each other. White Cap, Red Dog, and other important chiefs put their names to this treaty.

At this treaty, one of the chiefs, Ma-pa-chong (I am speaking Sioux)—he was the ninth chief to sign—asked La Bombarbe how it was that the bullets fired by the Indians made such small holes in the white men, and the white men's bullets made such large holes in the Indians. La Bombarbe said that was easily explained. It was because the Indians took the half-breeds unawares. They fired from afar. They were cowards. On the other hand, the half-breeds went up like men—the length of their guns—to the Indians. That explained the size of the bullet holes.

White Cap[3] was always a great friend of mine. He told me how the Minnesota massacre had come about. He said that seven young Sioux braves had gone from the Sioux camp (this was, of course, on American territory—before the Sioux came to Canada) to steal horses from the Chippewyans, who were camped at Red Lake, Minnesota.

Well, they did not succeed. They had to travel quite a long distance back to their camp at Devil's Lake. (This is Big Devil's Lake, Minnesota.) White Cap was at this camp then. These young Indians ran out of ammunition, and their food gave out. In a starving condition, they struck out for the nearest small settlement in Minnesota. They thought, "We will go into this camp and ask for something to eat." The oldest Indian in the brigade could speak a little English. He said he would go and ask for food. He knocked at the door. A woman opened it. She asked, in a rough voice, what he wanted. He told her that his brigade was starving, and asked her for some bread. She grabbed an axe and split his skull in two. Another brave tried to get into the house through a window. The woman killed him, too. She killed two of those warriors because of a piece of bread.

After these men were killed, the Sioux attacked the settlement. They killed all the settlers and burned the town. Everything was destroyed right down to the ground. I went through that settlement six months afterward with Bannatyne. The trail to Saint Paul led through it.

Those American Sioux were pretty fierce. Once forty of

3. Extract from *Manitoba Free Press*, May 21, 1885. *"White Cap."* "This is a Sioux, a very fine man, of tall stature, and gifted with highly intellectual qualities. He is a man of his word, and if he has promised alliance to Riel, he will follow him everywhere. He will go and place himself in the front of the cannons to obey him.

"In 1876, it was they who contributed the most to the defeat of General Crock. They were with Sitting Bull at the time of the Custer Massacre. They also took part in the campaign against General Miles. They are very gentle in character, and I think they are the best Indians in the North-west. They are considered the best warriors, and in prairie warfare, they are unequalled. There are not more than 250 in their band. If they have promised Riel to follow him, they will not be afraid to go meet the troops."

them, a band, came up from the American side, and attacked Batiste Framboise (Ah-you-skan), a half-breed hunter. They shot through his tent, killed his niece, and broke his daughter's leg in two places. Batiste said to his daughter, "Try and crawl away. I'll fight these beggars." Then he grabbed his gun and ammunition, and jumped out of his tent singing a war-song.

Framboise called out in Cree to these savages that he was going to use the devil's knife to kill their band. They got scared and ran, but he followed and killed quite a number of them. They were all warriors. Still, no matter how bold the Indian warriors were, they always feared the buffalo hunters, who were all dead shots, and quick to act. They could shoot an Indian, or anyone else for that matter, before he had time to think. This fight took place along the old Hudson's Bay trail that ran from Winnipeg westward. I picked up a skull belonging to one of those Sioux warriors on that trail, ran a stick through it, and hung it on a tree. It hung there for years.

CHAPTER TWENTY-THREE

I Find Myself under Arrest

My wife and children were surprised and glad to see me. News had come through that I had been shot. Next morning I went to the Fort. I went to Billy Sutherland's store. He was a member of the Legislature. He asked me if I had reported to the military authorities. There was a big camp of soldiers stationed at the Fort, with Captain O'Brien in charge. When I told Sutherland I had not reported, he said that he would go and report me. We went over to the camp.

When I told Captain O'Brien that all my supplies and stock had been seized by Riel, he asked what I was going to do. I told him I would get along somehow. Sutherland said, "No fear, Welsh will get along."

We went back to Sutherland's store. He asked me if I was in need of supplies; if so, I was to take what I wanted. I told him I had enough for the present, mentioning that I intended to go to Troy[1] next morning to get fifty bushels of seed oats.

We went out of the store. We saw a flag flying at half-mast from the Fort. We enquired about it, and found out that Captain French[2] had been shot at Batoche. Poor fellow, he had put his head out of the house to give a command and had been shot right through the mouth. Sutherland asked me if

---

1. Troy—Qu'Appelle.
2. Captain French, son of Sir George French, one time Governor of Australia.

I would bring two cases for him from Troy Station. He did not tell me what was in them. I agreed.

The next morning I started for Troy. I went right across country from Lebret. This way was shorter. I wanted to make the trip in one day. When I got to the station at Troy, Jones, a big fellow with a pot belly—I knew him very well—came and examined my load. I thought to myself, "You are a busybody," but I said nothing. I fastened my load well, lashed it tight.

Then I drove to the stables, put my horses up to feed, and got my dinner. I hadn't much time to lose, so I hurried and got on my way again. When I reached the Half-Way House, on the Hudson's Bay trail from Troy to Fort Qu'Appelle, I looked at the sun. It was nearly six o'clock. I thought I had better stop here for supper and feed my horses.

I went in and asked Mrs. Carroll if she could get me some supper in a hurry. She said I could have it right away. I ate my supper, paid for it, and went out to hook up my horses. I saw six mounted policemen coming at a gallop. I thought they must be after somebody. I finished hitching my horses, and put the reins on the tongue of the waggon.

The sergeant, a busy little fellow, rode up and asked whose outfit this was. I told him that it belonged to me, Norbert Welsh. He asked me what I had on board. I told him that he could see that I had oats, flour, and a side of bacon. He asked me what I had in the two cases at the bottom of my waggon. I told him I didn't know, that they belonged to Sutherland. I said, "You are camped right in front of his store. You must know him."

At that, he ordered me to unpack my load, take off the boxes, and open them. I told him if he wanted to see what was in the boxes, he could unpack the load, take off the cases, and open them himself. I said that I would not touch property that did not belong to me.

"You're quick with words," he said, "but you'll change your tune when you get to Captain O'Brien's camp."

"I will change my tune for no man," I told him.

He jumped off his horse, ordered his men to dismount

and overhaul my load. They took the two cases off, got an axe from Bill Carroll, and opened them. There were fourteen repeating rifles in one case, and the other case was full of cartridges. I said, "I must be a great warrior to have all that ammunition."

"We've got one of Riel's men!" they cried.

I told them I was ready to hook my horses onto the rig. The sergeant ordered me to get on my load. He said that his men would attach the traces and hand me the reins. Then he placed two mounted men ahead, two behind, and one on each side of me, and gave the signal to go.

"Hurrah for Welsh," I called. "You are doing me as much honor as if I were the Governor."

Again the sergeant told me I would not be so independent and proud of my name when I got to the police camp—to O'Brien. More than ever would I be proud of my name and extremely independent, I told him. As I said before, this sergeant was just a puppet of a man—no discernment. I let him go on. I wanted to bring him to humiliation. We travelled on.

After a while this little policeman ordered me to trot my team. I told him that the team was mine, that I would travel as I pleased. When we got to the top of the long hill that led to the Fort, I jumped off my rig to lock the waggon wheels to keep from running down the hill. My captor ordered me to get back on the waggon. His men, he said, would lock the wheels. I laughed, and said, "More honor for Welsh."

It was dark now. As we travelled through the village of Fort Qu'Appelle, I heard on every side cries of, "One of Riel's men is captured." We went right up to the door of O'Brien's tent. I jumped off my rig. Sutherland came running in with a lantern in his hand. He cried, "Oh, Welsh, I got you into trouble. I forgot to tell you what was in those cases."

I told him there would be no trouble. These policemen, you understand, were not the regular force; they were volunteers. The regular Royal North-West Mounted Policemen all knew and trusted me. More than that, they knew that if I had wanted to start a rebellion, all I had to do was to sound my whistle and Starblanket and all the other Indians would come to my assistance. I went to O'Brien.

"I am trusted and respected by all the men of the North-West, the Governor, Hudson's Bay officials, the Indians," I told him. "I reported here yesterday. It is too bad that a man in your position should have ordered my arrest. You should have a better memory. Now, I want you to give me a pass. I won't have Tom, Dick and Harry—" I pointed to the men who had brought me in—"stopping me on the trail." He did.

Next morning a policeman came galloping to my tent with a letter from O'Brien. I had the letter read, and in it O'Brien asked me to be at his camp at ten o'clock.

I said to my wife, "It would have been better if I had got into the rebellion, and shot a few dozen of these beggars, if they are going to follow me around like this."

I was not in a very pleasant mood. I ordered my man to throw a saddle on my fastest horse. I galloped to the Fort—to O'Brien's tent. He was busy and asked me to come back in ten minutes. I did.

I asked him what he wanted. He said there was a report that Starblanket and his band were getting ready to start a rebellion, and that he was going to stage a sham battle between Starblanket's Indians and his troops, just to scare the Indians. I warned him to watch out what he was about. Then he told me that he wanted me to make the arrangements, and to be there to take charge of the Indians because he knew I could control them.

The sham battle was arranged. The police and Starblanket's troops drew up and faced each other—one hundred yards apart. I told Starblanket that when the signal to advance was given, he should rush his men up against the police, but that he must not let them shoot. If any of his Indians showed signs of fighting in earnest, he must bang them on the head with the butt of his gun. Starblanket was a great leader. I knew that he could control his Indians.

The order was given. The Indians made a wild rush. The policemen—as I have said before, they were greenhorns—

bolted. They were terrified at the sight of the advancing Indians.

O'Brien couldn't say anything. He treated the Indians well. He gave them tea, flour, sugar and tobacco. This sham battle took place on the flats, where the Pioneer store now stands.

Gabriel Dumont was one of Riel's active generals right through, but he was no man to organize a fighting outfit. At no time did he have the Métis and Indian warriors properly under control. Of course he and his troops put Middleton's soldiers back at Fish Creek, and that was good as they were not as well armed as their opponents, but after that he seemed to lose his head. He gained nothing by bringing Riel back. What I predicted came true. In the end he had to leave the country.

Middleton was a fellow who had a great opinion of himself. The war he was sent out to conduct was not a war at all, but a kind of bush skirmish with his men scattered all over the place. Captain Howard, an American officer, who had fought in the army in the American West was a good leader. After the Fish Creek defeat, he was rushed in to show the soldiers how to handle the Gatling guns. He was anxious to go against the American Sioux chief, White Cap, and his band, as they were refugees from Minnesota where they had scalped a great many women and children. Howard was very businesslike, the men said.

Of course Major Steele and Herchmer of the Police were the right men to put down Riel's uprising, and they did, though Middleton got the credit and twenty thousand dollars from the Government. At "Stand Up Coulee," so named because Big Bear made a stand here, Steele put his forty-six men against Big Bear's six hundred warriors and beat the Indians back. In the end, too, he split up Big Bear's band, and the Chief had to let his white prisoners go free. Steele and Herchmer were men who could lead. They knew how to command. And they knew the country.

Tom Hourie was the man that took Riel prisoner. The

account of Riel's hanging in Regina is well known. It almost split the country apart. I have had the speech Sir Wilfrid Laurier made about it in the House of Commons read to me. The whole thing was too bad.

My poor friend, Poundmaker, who kept his people from joining Riel, gave himself up to Middleton, but not with humility. He had no humility, that man. I can never think that Poundmaker wanted to join Riel. He was a great Chief. The poor fellow! He was sent to prison. The one favor he asked his captors was that they should not cut off his long black braids. When he came out of prison he hadn't a horse left on his reservation. He walked to Alberta—to the camp of his foster-father, Chief Crowfoot of the Blackfoot tribe. This was a distance of about three hundred and fifty miles. He had a fever and a cough. He took small doses of painkiller, which was a remedy the Indians used to buy from the traders for their sicknesses. Four months after his release from prison, Poundmaker died in Crowfoot's camp of a hemorrhage from the lung.

The rebellion put me back. I lost everything I had at the time. After a time everything quieted down in the North-West.

CHAPTER TWENTY-FOUR

Rancher and Business Man

fter that there was no further trouble. I advised Starblanket to keep his Indians quietly at home. His men listened to him. Some of the bands, however, were restless. They were not satisfied with the way things were going on the Reserve. But Starblanket managed them. He was a great leader. I noticed that O'Brien didn't offer to put on any more exhibitions of war. He had had enough. Very shortly after that Riel was captured, and the rebellion was over. In the end Gabriel Dumont didn't think he was so clever. He had to flee to United States territory where he would be safe.

After the rebellion, I stayed at Lebret for a while until things quieted down. Nobody knew yet what the Indians would do. They were still pretty nervous. But, I will say this for them: they had fine chiefs, who were sensible and reasonable men. It is a pity that some of the civilized men of that time hadn't as much sense as the savage Indian Chiefs. Well, anyway, I decided to stay quiet for a while. I had to decide what I would do for a living now. I used all my influence with the bands—they were still muttering—to keep them quiet. Gradually the unrest died out, and there was no more talk of war.

Then I got ready and moved north to what is now Jasmine, and took up a cattle ranch. I had lost everything in the rebellion, remember, and had to start at the beginning again. I started with a few head of cattle and gradually increased my stock. I got a little money ahead, and I began to get ambitious again. I began bringing in pure bred stock from Winnipeg and England. My stock—and it was fine stock—increased. I made money.

After a while I began to think about trading again. That was my business. I had a fine boodle of money by this time, so I decided to buy a ranch near the File Hills Indian Agency and start a store. There was no store between the Agency and the Hudson's Bay Post at Fort Qu'Appelle. All the business of the Indians was going to the Fort. The Indians had plenty of furs, small furs of course, but fine furs. I could not endure seeing all this business escape me. I decided to waste no more time on this ranch.

I hitched up and drove to the File Hills and had a good look around. I sized the thing up, you might say. My Indians were very much pleased to see me! Well, I bought a ranch—it was fine ranching country around the Reserve—near the Indian Agency. I wanted this for my pure-blood stock, for there was plenty of free grazing land all around. My stock would have a fine grazing range—thousands of miles of unoccupied land.

I got moved, and the first thing I did was to put up quite a good-sized store. I fixed everything up first-class. Then I stocked up with all kinds of goods. My shelves were filled with everything that would please the Indians. I had flour, tea, sugar, tobacco, all kinds of dried fruits, groceries, prints, calicoes, beads—fine beads that came from England and Germany—lots of vermilion, tobacco, shot, powder—everything that the Hudson's Bay Company sold. You see, I had made up my mind to get all my Indian trade. I did. And my Indians were very happy!

Then I began to trade. Although there were no more buffalo robes to be had, there were all kinds of small furs. Starblanket and his band, and the half-breeds from all over, brought me the very finest skins, all tanned to perfection. Starblanket and his people were our best customers. They brought muskrat, wolf, lynx, bear, marten, weasel, badger, skunk, and the skins of a little animal that looked like a badger. It was called petite chien-de-prairie (prairie-dog).

These prairie-dog skins were very special. They were very much like skunk.

One day I took in five hundred dollars in furs alone—in trade, remember. I made a profit on my goods, and another profit on furs. I doubled my money on each transaction. On another day, my wife—I had gone to Fort Qu'Appelle—took in seven hundred fine muskrat skins. She paid two and a half cents apiece for them in trade. These skins were well stretched. Some of them measured about eight inches across. My wife chose ten of the largest of these skins—they were an odd grey shade—and sent them to her mother who lived in Winnipeg. My mother-in-law took them to the Hudson's Bay Company Post at Fort Garry. The Chief factor, Donald A. Smith[1] (later Lord Strathcona and Mount Royal)—he was the last factor—thought them so unusual that he kept them on display at the Fort for a long time. Finally, he bought them from my mother-in-law and had them made into a set of furs for his daughter. It was thought that these furs were a cross between a muskrat and some other animal. They were a great curiosity.

In addition to buying seven hundred muskrat skins that day, my wife took in also twelve badger skins at fifty cents apiece, five mink skins at seventy-five cents each, and twenty-four weasel skins at ten cents each.

I sold all my furs to Archibald MacDonald, Chief Factor at Fort Qu'Appelle. For the muskrat skins, I got six cents apiece, for the badger two dollars and a half apiece, for the mink five dollars each, and for the weasel skins twenty-five cents each.

I bought all kinds of moccasins from the Indians. They were handsome moccasins, embroidered in all colors, and trimmed with weasel fur—ermine. They were of different styles. Some were made with tops, while others were slippers. The Indians brought them to me in big packs of twenty-four

1. "Prior to and at the time of the demolition of the Fort, Donald A. Smith was Chief Commissioner for the Company in North America, with head-quarters at Fort Garry, and later the newer premises at Winnipeg."

or forty-eight pairs lashed together with shaggannappi. I paid from fifty cents a pair up for them, according to the quality. Those for which I paid fifty cents, I sold for from a dollar and a quarter to a dollar and a half, depending on the style and amount of decoration. The Hudson's Bay Company bought all my moccasins. Some were sold in this country, and some were shipped to England.

At first I had freighters haul all my goods from Winnipeg. Then I had them shipped by rail to Troy (now Qu'Appelle)—the railroad was now at Troy—and hauled them from there. This was a long distance to haul goods. MacDonald paid me a good price for my furs, and he had the very best of goods. MacDonald and I came to an agreement about the prices, and after that I bought all my merchandise and stuff from, or through, him at the Fort Qu'Appelle trading-post. There were no finer men in the country than the Hudson's Bay Company's factors. The Hudson's Bay Company was noted in this country, first for the quality of its men, and second, for the quality of its goods.

Meanwhile I kept on ranching just the same. I kept improving my stock, buying more pure bred cattle all the time. I had a garden, too, and raised feed for my stock. I raised no wheat. It was new ground and rich, but there were lots of stones. My vegetables did well. One year I raised a turnip that was too big to go into a milk pail. It weighed thirty-two pounds.

I made a lot of money from stock alone. A neighbor, J.E. Johnson—he was married to Captain French's daughter—imported an English Shire horse—a stallion—from England at a cost of about two thousand, five hundred dollars landed at the Ranch. His name was Granite—I got some of my heavy stock from him. I raised, sold, and traded both thoroughbred horses and cattle. I had one fine bay stallion. He was a son of Derwentwater, the famous horse that was imported into this country from England by Mr. Lawson. Derwentwater was shown at the Madison Square Horse Show, New York, and won the Championship for Thoroughbred Stallions. He had won several championships in the old country. I had this horse Derwentwater Chief for some years, then I sold him for nine hundred dollars. I sold another team for five hundred dollars. That was the way things went. I made money on every side. Little did I think, in those days, that I would become blind and helpless and have to accept an old-age pension. If we only knew enough to save our money! My stock being fat and of good breed, buyers came from as far as Winnipeg for my cattle. I shipped steers and heifers by the carload.

I stayed at File Hills until 1904. By this time settlers had crowded around and had taken up all the land. My cattle range became restricted. Furs were becoming scarce too. I sold out. I had a hundred and fifty acres, I sold it for twenty-five dollars an acre.

Next I came back here to Lebret. The old free life of the plains was over. I put up a shop. It was a store and butcher shop combined. I had kept six teams of my best driving horses, and I began to run a livery between Lebret and Troy (Qu'Appelle). We did a fine business. Money was coming from all over. Then the railroad, the Grand Trunk, came to Fort Qu'Appelle and our business was, you might say, ended. I lost my eyesight in 1916. If I had my eyesight I could still make money. Instead, I am obliged to sit here and review in my mind the passing of the old West.

I like best to remember the exciting buffalo hunts. I think, too, of the long caravans of Red River carts that started out yearly from Fort Garry to cross the plains to the forks of the lordly Saskatchewan River. How our voices carried over the quiet plains as we sang the old songs of the trail! I can remember every one of them. I will sing one for you. It is called, "Les Adieux."

CHAPTER TWENTY-FIVE

Songs of the Buffalo Hunters

The Red River traders, who started out yearly from the Hudson's Bay post at Fort Garry outfitted with goods to trade to the Indians for furs and to themselves hunt buffalo on the Canadian plains, were an artistic as well as a light-hearted and courageous people. All their impressions were recorded in song.

On their long trips westward over the prairies, the leader of the brigade lifted his voice in a high, clear note. Instantly the tune rang down the long, swaying line of carts, and straightway the musical voices of the prairie voyageurs drowned the doleful wailing of the Red River carts.

Community singing was in vogue on the prairie then as now. Groups of buffalo hunters, with their families, and friends, met around camp fires of buffalo chips on the open prairie to dry their buffalo meat, to make pemmican, to mend their harnesses and carts, and to listen to each other's musical compositions. Or after perilous buffalo hunts, at holiday festivities held at wintering houses in the heart of the Indian country, to commemorate births, marriages, and deaths, they met to express themselves in song. A tune was chosen. Then words to fit the air, whether to record joyful or bitter experiences, were wrung from their hearts.

Most of the old Trader songs have been forgotten. Strangers, English folk mostly, have set up towns and cities and built long straight roads across the prairie where once the buffalo grazed and the hunters of the plains criss-crossed the trails on their tuneful way. Modern songs, jazz mainly, have supplanted the plaintive tunes of the buffalo hunters of an age just past. Here are a few of the old songs which have survived.

A Comic Song

1. When I was very little I was not very tall,
    When I was very little I was not so tall,
    At fifteen I dated with the pretty lassies all.
    >   Hia ha ha that will not do!
    >   Hia ha ha that will not do!
    >   Hia ha ha that will not do!
    >   Hia ha ha that will not do!

2. At fifteen I dated with the pretty lassies all, (twice)
    And on a stool I climbed to kiss, I was so small.
    >   Hia ha ha that will not do! (four times)

3. And on a stool I climbed to kiss, I was so small. (twice)
    One day I saw my mother come running in a rage.
    >   Hia ha ha that will not do! (four times)

4. One day I saw my mother come running in a rage,
    (twice)
    "Run home, you little rascal, you've not earned that wage!"
    >   Hia ha ha that will not do! (four times)

5. "Run home, you little rascal, you've not earned that wage! (twice)
    You can call on girls, sir, when of maturer age!"
    >   Hia ha ha that will not do! (four times)

6. "You can call on girls, sir, when of maturer age!"
    (twice)
    Meseems, 'twill be a long time ere I reach that state!!!
    >   Hia ha ha that will not do! (four times)

Love in English

Won't you, in your English advancing,
Learn just a few new words each day?
Forgive me, my one well-beloved,
If I find a fault in some way;
Ofttimes, when my poor heart is sighing
Quite well do you know "c'est pour vous."
　　　　　　　　　　'tis for you.
I only am he who may whisper—
"Je vous aim-e, vous, ne que vous."
I love you, yes you, only you.

But love has oft misunderstandings,
"Chaque pays" just as with you.
May all these clear in happy endings,
As each confesses "Love is true."
Just yester-night you were so angry
I feared my dearest hope was lost,
But if I once a-gain may please you,
I love, I shall not count the cost!

You soon will see, my sweet adored one,
"En Anglais" love is not for mirth,
Not I, a fashion-able lover
I'm just a human man on Earth,
My only fashion is love's method
A very tender earnest plea.
I beg that you will answer "Yes dear"
When I say "Prithee marry me!"

The Two Hearts

1. *SHE.* "My fate is O so hard since I am forced to still
　　My heart's love deeply hidden in a convent
　　　　'gainst my will.
　　I'll break, I think, my chain

To see my lover dear.
He is a smart young Captain,
And my heart desires him here."

2. "Turtle dove, pray bear him, wherever he may be,
   This little note, these words, from one who
       loves him tenderly."
   The dove took the letter
   Her beak those sweet words pressed
   To thicket green she bore it
   And she hid it in her nest.

3. Thrice the lover, knocking, desired his mistress dear,
   And thrice the convent gate refused him, the
       portress made it clear.

PORTRESS. "You must not reproach her,
   You may not ever meet.
   Her mother's kinsmen brought her,
   Fearing Love's long-hidden heat.
   To-day she has received her early pledge of Heaven,
   Withdraw, nor seek to break the vow already given."

4. *HE.* "Fainting at thy threshold,
   O hear at least my cry,
   Keep thou thy sacred promise,
   'Tis all that I may, I die!"

The lovers are parted, the bird fails as messenger. The maid reluctantly makes her convent vow. The lover, who is too late, respects the vow and parts from life.

Old Wedding Song

1. To-day is the dawn of my wedding morning,
   The happiest day of my life I ween.

Refrain:
"Yes, yes, my dearest, I love thee,
Shall I not be forever thine own?"
(twice)

2. Let me take for a moment that kerchief white,
   Its purity gains from thy virginal touch.

3. Give me but one glass of the festival wine,
   To slake the hot fire in my burning throat.

4. Goodbye, my friends, and all my kith and kindred,
   I leave perforce, but I will soon return.

5. Just before parting, O family so dear,
   I would thank you for your tenderness to me.

6. Virgin Mother! bless those espoused souls,
   Guard them o'er the trail of Life to Journey's end!

Bridegroom—dramatizing his words, 1, 2, 3, and refrain, to the bride; 4, 5, to the assembly. 6 appears to be farewell prayer to the assembly for bride and groom. Probably this in time became a well-known song sung by all around the happy pair.

The Grandmother's Song

1. I dreamed when young my girlish dreams,
   A joyous future planning,
   And hoped in marriage I would find
   A bridge that future spanning.
   I hear life's strain more plainly,
   For marriage is no key for love,
   It is a discord mainly.
   My tune has changed since those bright days.

2. I always thought my wedding day
   Would bring me joy abiding,
   But now I see those weary chains

Which love had held in hiding.
In those young days I was right gay,
My lot was bright and cheerful,
Amid my friends my days were passed,
My griefs were never tearful.

3. A suitor came on bended knee,
    For my cold hand beseeching,
    Convinced my father of his love,
    Prepared to give me teaching.
    He swore to love me all his days,
    Honor, protect and guard me,
    He said, "My fair one, let me hope
    Against all else to ward thee."

4. My father, pleased with lover's vows,
    Said, "Thus I'll keep her near me.
    They'll both be mine, I shall not lack
    In old age love to cheer me."
    Ah, yes, in faith, my husband loves,
    But I am free no longer.
    I may not peep at life outside,
    His jealousy grows stronger.

5. 'Tis hard to think a father's love,
    Seeking to make life pleasant,
    Has failed to buy the simple peace
    Which dowers a lowly peasant.
    He wished to find a tenderness
    To charm my days with loving.
    He found a love, a jealous pride,
    To watch lest mine go roving.

6. I must in solitude spend hours,
    Hot tears for lost life shedding,
    This loneliness my portion is,
    Not flowery paths a-treading.

Almost grim Death I would prefer,
He'd loose each jealous fetter.
Or else, kind Heaven! Change my man,
That really might be better.

The grandmother tells how the old French system in which papa chose
the husband failed to bring promised happiness. The husband was jealous,
her home a prison. Her father's plans miscarried. Married possibly at
sixteen, her son or daughter married at the same age, she might herself
have been only in her early thirties at the time of writing, or composing, her
spirited song.